NEW LIFE
CLARITY
PUBLISHING

New Life Clarity Publishing
205 West 300 South, Brigham City, Utah 84302

Https://newlifeclarity.com/

Printed in the United States of America

ISBN- 978-1-0878-5796-1

THE VIRTUITY EDGE

From Ordinary to Extraordinary

By: Hanna L. Horenstein

FOREWARD

For years I've talked about the establishment versus the movement. As a founding member of my Arete Syndicate and a visionary in the financial services and personal and leadership development areas, Hanna and her Virtuity family are leading the movement against the establishment. They have become a force majeure in influencing and creating change by uniting those with and without money to a common goal of financial education, information and awareness among all communities.

Ed Mylett ~ Entrepreneur, Public Figure,
Top 50 wealthiest under 50, Best Selling Author,
Fitness Addict, Global Speaker, Co-Founder Arete Syndicate

~~~

Financial education is the gift of a lifetime. Virtuity Financial Partners provide information and education to individuals, business owners and families on how to take control of their finances and create real, long-term and immediate change in their lives.

Sharon Lechter CPA CGMA, Author of
Think and Grow Rich for Women, Co-author of
Outwitting the Devil, Three Feet From Gold,
Rich Dad Poor Dad and 14 other Rich Dad books.

~~~

As a shark on "shark tank" I had an opportunity to work with many companies and many teams. Working with Hanna and her team at Virtuity has been refreshing and fun. They have created a space for entrepreneurs and influencers at any level to help either start a business, add a much needed additional income stream, and most importantly help people of all walks of life get access to financial education.

Kevin Harrington, An original "shark" on the hit TV show *Shark Tank*, the creator of the infomercial, pioneer of the As Seen on TV brand, and co-founding board member of the *Entrepreneur's Organization*—Kevin Harrington has pushed past all the questions and excuses to repeatedly enjoy 100X success. His legendary work behind-the-scenes of business ventures has produced well over $5 billion in global sales, the launch of more than 500 products, and making dozens of millionaires. Twenty of his companies have each topped $100 million in revenue.

~~~

This book shows you how you can start and build a highly profitable business. It is filled with inspirational stories that will help motivate you to kick-start your success. I highly recommend this book for anyone wanting more out of life and wanting to achieve wealth. Plain and simple, if you want to succeed as an entrepreneur, this book will give you the opportunity to put yourself on the road to riches.

Omar Periu, Author of
The Smart Start-Up, Get Real Get Rich,
From Zero to Wealth, The One-Minute Meeting,
***Get Fired Up,* and many more.**

~~~

The Price of success is hard work, dedication, and determination to the job at hand. Never giving up which allows one to apply their very best and accomplish their set goals. Hanna and every associate in this book have committed to this as a standard accepting nothing less.

Marshall Faulk, *NFL HALL OF FAMER,*
Entrepreneur, Marketing Director with Virtuity/WFG

ACKNOWLEDGEMENT

Thank you God for blessing us with this incredible life. I'm eternally grateful to Jamie and Shawn Villalovos for introducing me to this path and coaching me continuously through good times and bad. Also to John and Arlene Shin who not only trained me when I was a rookie but also welcomed me into their home as family. Both couples have served as incredible examples of success not only in business, but as a family. I also give credit to a business coach by the name of Sam Lin, who helped me tremendously in my early days. This coaching was invaluable.

Other mentors that have shaped who I am as a person today, and have provided incredible support and direction as well as becoming great friends are: Dan and Sophia Charlier; Ed and Kristianna Mylett; Bill and Peggy Mitchell; Jeff and Cam Levitan; Greg and Tina Kapp; Rich and Cindy Thawley; Monte and Lisa Holm; Elan and Dina Michael; Rob and Tiffany Day and countless others: Thank you all for helping me shape my mindset and inspiring me to become the best possible businesswoman I could be.

I am beyond thankful for our team, Virtuity. I am thankful for our top leaders featured in this book, and every single member of our team. Without the tireless efforts of our team, Virtuity would not exist.

I am thankful for my entire family, who support me as I've worked to build my business. My husband David for his continuing support and hard work that he gives. My children Shayna and Ely for believing in us and the biggest reason why we do what we do. My sister Galit and my parents Irina and Benjamin for the lessons I've learned through life.

I truly believe this is just the beginning and there are many more years of hard work and success to come for our team.

I thank WFG and our home office employees for giving us the opportunity that we have to build a business that allows us to achieve all that we can be and do.

Finally, thank you so very much to those who wrote their forewords to add to this book. I feel blessed beyond measure to have your support. It is from influential people like you who have inspired me to reach for greatness in my own life.

DEDICATION

*To those who would aspire
to reach greater heights and
achieve success with a passion to
serve others.*

About The Author

Hanna Horenstein has been a licensed financed advisor for nearly two decades. She has coached and mentored individuals and families from all walks of life, including celebrities, athletes, business owners and many families just starting out. She has offices all throughout Southern California and continues to expand across the United states. With a team of over 400 licensed associates throughout the nation, her guidance and experience has encouraged families and individuals to take control of their financial situation and pursue success.

TABLE OF CONTENTS

1. The Story Of Virtuity..1

2. Hanna L. Horenstein..3

3. Rudy Lasry..23

4. Gene Coppa..33

5. Grant Wright..41

6. Joseph Gopez..49

7. Sara Rose Macias..55

8. Shkira Singh..65

9. Oliver And Jaimie Ziman..69

10. Jen Madamba-Bailey..75

11. David Bailey..81

12. Ben Klinger..87

13. Sharon Griffin..95

14. Lester Baron..103

15. Kirsten Baron 109

16. Carlos Rojas 117

17. Yvette Rojas 121

18. Raul Julian Reyes, Jr. 129

THE STORY OF VIRTUITY

This is the question that I am asked at least several times per day. My answer is two faceted. The name is a combination of the words *virtuous* and *infinity*. In other words, you should always be virtuous in all of your dealings. The second facet of the name has an origin of continued growth. Growth in all that you aspire to be, aspire to do, aspire to create, and with a basis that stems from a platform of integrity.

The reason for this book being written is to give you, the reader an "inside" look as to who Virtuity is and hear firsthand from some of the people who have helped shape the culture, success and current trajectory of Virtuity.

"Virtuity is a co-brand. The name is a way to differentiate our team from the sea of almost sixty thousand agents in one of the most fascinating companies I've ever seen, World Financial Group.

Virtuity is a team that has come together over a span of twenty years. We are a team that is made up of individuals aligned with a common purpose. That purpose is to right the wrong of the current financial industry. Our mission is to share financial literacy and entrepreneurship with the masses of people, that for too long have worked under a system designed to fail.

What we do is educate people. We make them aware of their current state of being when it comes to their finances and lifestyle by walking them through a financial needs analysis. We encourage them to explore their goals and dreams, and create a "Dream Life Picture." Once that Picture is in their mind, then we guide them in the creation of a step by step roadmap, to reach that dream of where they want to be, from where they are now.

In this book, you the reader, will have an opportunity to become familiar with some of our top leaders. These leaders have been with Virtuity, anywhere from two years to twenty years.

You will read their stories of how they started; when they started; when they had their "AH-HA" moment; and their plans for the future. You'll also read about the challenges they've had to overcome. You will read of their struggles, battles, and ultimately their victory. You will learn how they became leaders in the family culture of Virtuity.

If you the reader feel compelled to reach out to any one of these leaders, you will find their personal email addresses and phone numbers listed in this book. Our ultimate goal is to extend to everyone, the opportunity that those of us at Virtuity enjoy. We invite people and families that can and will benefit from learning and joining the Virtuity movement.

Hanna L. Horenstein

I was born in Toronto, Canada to Russian/Israeli parents, and when I was eight, we moved to the U.S. My parents were never educated about how money works, and although throughout my childhood they did well financially (we were considered upper middle class), they still never learned the rules of how to grow money, save money, and protect it. They only knew how to earn it.

When we moved to Los Angeles in the early 1980s, they

had approximately $500,000 in cash, and at the time, that was a lot of money. They purchased our home with cash and used cash to pay for both of their cars. It might sound like a smart idea to pay with cash, so as not to go into debt, but sometimes having all your eggs in one basket can be unwise.

We moved many times due to my father's work in real estate development, and we usually moved into homes they had improved before he "flipped" the house for profit. For several years, this strategy worked quite well for them; until we had our first recession. Since all of their metaphorical eggs were in one basket (i.e., real estate), I watched my parents lose our home to foreclosure. We went from living in large and beautiful homes to living in a 900-square-foot apartment.

I learned from this experience that no matter how good things look today, you always need to prepare for unforeseen circumstances that might occur. No matter what happens, be it an act of God, a recession, or a change in health for you or a loved one, it is imperative that you have a plan.

After the apartment, we hopscotched from home to home one last time, and then it was time for college. I will never forget asking my parents where I should apply, and my dad telling me, "You can go anywhere you want: UC Valley or UC Pierce!" Those happen to be two local community colleges that don't cost much. What he was really trying to tell me was that he hadn't saved any money for my college education.

My parents never taught me anything about saving money, and money itself was never discussed in our home. But as a child, there are several things I picked up on. For example, once my father took me to the grocery store, and a newspaper salesman kept trying to sell him a subscription. My father said no and walked away. Done. Simple as that.

But the salesman persisted. "Sir," he said, "what do you do for a living?"

"I am self-employed," my father replied.

As we walked away from the salesman, I felt horrified. "Dad," I asked, "why did you tell him we were poor?"

"I didn't say we were *poor.*"

"Yes," I insisted, "you told that man you didn't have a job!"

"That is correct," my father replied with a hint of pride in his voice. "I *don't* work for anyone else; I work for myself. I own my *own* business."

That was the first time I realized that you didn't need to work for anyone else to succeed. And you could, in fact, "be your own boss." I liked that idea as I've always had a hard time being told what to do.

From age 11 to 18, I must have had somewhere between twenty to thirty different jobs. I was let go from each job after being told I needed to do something that I didn't want to do, like mopping the floors at a juice bar. I thought my job was just making juice!

I also had a very hard time in school. My GPA hovered around 2.0 most of the time, and sometimes dropped below that. Knowing I couldn't hold a job, and after barely graduating from high school, I was very happy to learn that I still had a chance in life.

I ended up doing about five years of community college. I earned my real estate license at the bright young age of 18. I submitted for my final exam on my eighteenth birthday. I had spent the last six months in real estate training school, studying for that exam, and I passed!

It just goes to show that if you're excited about doing something, make a decision and just go for it! Although I was an average student in college, earning mostly C's and D's, I aced my real estate exam on the first try because I finally made up my mind to just *go for it.* Nothing is more powerful than a made-up mind. I entered the real estate business excited, and ready and willing to work hard.

Once I landed my first real estate job, what was presented to me was a phonebook and a script. I was told to "dial for dollars," which turns out is not as easy as I had hoped. On top of that, it was 1995, and we had just experienced the great Northridge earthquake. The homes in the San Fernando Valley were either underwater or condemned, and nobody wanted to sell.

My friends were all 18-19 years old at the time, and they couldn't afford to buy a house. I ended up working several part-time jobs while trying to sell real estate, and I did what so many people end up doing when they are trying to get by: I started using credit cards.

About 2 years into my unsuccessful real estate career, I was approached by a friend of mine who had an unbelievable idea to market to successful realtors by taking their listings and hosting a "virtual tour." This sounded like a great idea. The Internet was starting to take off at that time.

As it turned out, we ended up growing very fast, and as soon as we were ready to cash our first check, one of our partners decided purely for his own ego that he wanted to become president, having done none of the work we had done in order to actually build the company. This blew up the company, and we shut down after just one year in business. That was one of the hardest things I've ever had to go through, as I thought this was our chance to "hit it big."

Three years into my real estate career, and all I had to show for it was one failed business. I remember feeling humbled when I had to take a telemarketing job at a bank/mortgage company that paid $10.00 per hour. I felt like I had hit rock bottom. I had a ton of credit card debt and no hope for the future. I remember three separate people approaching me with a "message from God," telling me I needed to get my life together and get on the right path because "I was meant to do big things."

After spending some time in the mortgage business, I realized I wanted to explore that field further. I wanted to progress and move farther up the ladder, but the company wanted me to work five years as a junior loan officer (fancy name for telemarketer) before I could become a senior loan officer. That was ridiculous. So I found a mortgage company that was set up like a brokerage, and I was able to start immediately as a senior loan officer.

The problem was that I was still self-employed, I had no training, and I was essentially told to find people that needed a loan and then the broker would help. The difference here was that we had over twenty different banks sending rate sheets, and I was able to serve my clients' needs rather than "sell" the client what my bank offered.

I learned a lot that year. I also earned quite a bit of money for a 22-year-old (about 60k), which was more than I had ever earned at that time. What I also remember is that every time a loan was in the process of closing, I was stressed and panicked, and then relieved when it closed.

Following the closure of each loan, I was essentially unemployed again, looking for the next deal. I loved it, but I also hated it. Mortgage sales/commissions is like chasing a high. Once it's over, you're dead in the water again. The last loan I closed at that company almost fell through, and I remember praying for something to change. It was at that time that a good friend of mine, Jaime Villalovos, left our mortgage company only one month after starting. She had been recruited into a completely different industry.

I was curious, to say the least, as to what amazing opportunity could have possibly lured her away from what I saw as a very lucrative mortgage company. She simply told me to come to some sort of seminar on a Saturday morning.

At this time, I spent my evenings promoting clubs, mostly for fun; but it was also supplementing my income. I was paid a dollar amount for every person I got on a list, as long as they showed up. This meant I was out late Thursday, Friday and Saturday nights, and the idea of showing up to an early Saturday morning seminar did *not* appeal to me. My friend shrugged and told me, "Well, then I guess you're really not interested in knowing what I'm doing." I felt challenged. I felt determined to prove her wrong. I showed up to that Saturday morning meeting. And it's a good thing I did because, although I didn't realize it at the time, that was the day my life changed forever.

I walked into an office in Tarzana on Ventura Blvd. There were probably around thirty to forty people in that room, and I sat in the very back. There was a speaker in front of us talking about all things financial. I was 22 and totally broke, and I remember thinking that this really wasn't for me.

I still loved the real estate and mortgage business, and I had no desire to go into any other field. I remember falling asleep in the back of the room and most of the information went right over my head. I woke up just in time to see the most important slide in the presentation: a slide called "The Rule of 72."

The presenter said something about how Einstein once said that this rule was the eighth wonder of the World. Apparently *this* was the way money compounded. I still didn't understand this, and the presenter said plainly, "This is how you double your money." That idea sounded intriguing, of course, but I had about six dollars saved in my bank account.

I thought this idea sounded interesting but didn't think it could apply to me. That was when the speaker said, "This rule applies to people in debt as well." He went on to explain that if you took the interest rate you're paid on, or the interest rate you are being charged, and you divide it into seventy-two, you can determine the number of years it will take your money, or debt, to double.

At that time, I had approximately $30,000 in debt at close to 30%. I did the math in my head and figured that I was paying $9,000 per year in interest just to hold onto my $30,000 in debt. Everything I ever paid for via credit card started flashing in my head: meals, drinks, Las Vegas trips, clothes I didn't need, furniture, and junk I didn't really need to decorate my apartment. If you give a kid access to money, but never teach them how to use it, you're essentially giving them a loaded gun to play with.

At the time I was paying $500.00 per month, which is what I had budgeted to pay off my credit cards. That meant

I was paying $6,000.00 per year, even though I was charged $9,000.00 per year in interest. I was going deeper and deeper into debt, and I didn't even know it! The speaker said you need to earn high rates of return on the money you're saving and pay low rates on the money you're borrowing. I was doing the complete opposite. And the even bigger issue was that I was not saving money at all! I had never heard of these principles before. In all those years of going to school (5 years in college, 4 years in high school, 17 years living with my parents, 2 years in real estate, 1 year in business ownership, and 1 year in mortgage), somehow I had never learned how money worked.

Once you see something, you can't unsee it. So now at 22 years old, I remember thinking *I am broke, I am failing at this money thing, and I am not doing anything to change it.* I remember thinking that I was not interested in going into financial services as a career, but I knew I definitely needed someone to help me with my own finances.

At that seminar, I met a man named John Shin. He sat me down and asked me three important questions. He asked, "In your current business of real estate, who makes more money, the broker or the agent?"

After a long pause, I guessed. "...The broker?"

"Who do you want to be?" he asked. "The broker, or the agent?"

The broker, obviously, but none of my previous brokers had ever told me they wanted to help me do what they did and earn what they earned. How could I run an office like they did? How could I truly run a successful business, given that I had a failed one under my belt?

John asked his second question. "Every time you close a transaction, sell a home, or close a loan, how many times do you get paid on that transaction?"

"Um…" I mumbled. "Once?"

"So you mean to tell me," he said, "that you're not earning residual income?"

Residual income. I had never heard that term before, and I hadn't the slightest idea what it meant.

John continued. "When a musician releases a song, he gets paid every time it plays, right? You do the work one time, and it pays you over and over again."

The third question he asked was, "If you walk around the mall right now and randomly ask people how many of them are ready to buy, sell, or refinance a home today, how many people do you think would say yes?"

I admitted to him that it would be very few, as that was currently an issue for me as well.

"How many of those people need to get out of debt, save more money, analyze or purchase additional insurance coverage, save money for their kids' college, pay less in taxes in retirement, or even earn additional income?"

"Probably everyone," I said.

At that moment, I started realizing what an incredible opportunity this was, and I decided to become an associate with the group. As it turned out, this was just the beginning of what was going to be a long journey.

Despite my initial enthusiasm, I still feared this might be a scam of some kind. When they asked me for $100 to become a member, that made me uncomfortable. Why did they want me to give them one hundred dollars to work there? What kind of "opportunity" was this anyway?

My problem was, I was still thinking like an employee. I didn't understand that in order to start a business, you need to spend money first. I later learned that this was because I was never going to have any ownership in any of those companies, and I was simply a salesperson, not the entrepreneur I always dreamed of becoming. So I bit the bullet and paid the one hundred dollars. I started attending training sessions where I was encouraged to start bringing friends, family, or people that I thought might have potential in this industry. This was probably both the easiest and hardest thing I've had to do.

My friends were happy to check out these seminars, but almost every single one laughed at me and thought I was crazy. They told me I was part of a cult, or that I'd gotten sucked into some kind of pyramid scheme. I felt offended by that, and many of those friends stopped speaking to me.

I've always had a lot of friends, all of whom were ready to go out with me and party the night away. But suddenly the music stopped, and everyone treated me like I contracted a contagious disease, just because I was trying to improve my life, learn a new business, and share it with my friends. On top of that, I was still very much afraid that this was in fact a scam and that I was being taken for a ride.

Despite my misgivings, I decided to keep moving forward. I attended meetings and training seminars, and I brought whoever I could convince to tag along. None of my friends joined me in the business, but one of the agents at my previous mortgage company decided to join as well as someone who was part of my clubbing days and who had just graduated from UCSB.

By the time our real first event happened, I had been in the business for about eight months and was still very skeptical. I had two business partners attending the event with me. I had been told this was an event I absolutely couldn't afford to miss, but I was so deep in debt that I couldn't pay for the two-hundred-dollar ticket.

John Shin, who was now my mentor, said, "You already have thirty-thousand dollars in credit card debt, so what's another two hundred? At least this is for something that can help you understand our business." He encouraged me to go, and if I didn't learn what I hoped to learn, he told me he would reimburse me for the money I spent. I decided to go. I decided I would go to Las Vegas, have fun at the clubs, then come back, get his reimbursement and then quit this company altogether! It sounded like a win-win.

I drove to Las Vegas with my two business partners and missed the entire first day of the event due to our late-night partying. The second day, Arlene Shin, John's wife, sent me a text asking where I was. It was noon and I wasn't where I was supposed to be. I showed up around one. I didn't plan on participating in the event; I was only going just to say I had. What I didn't know at that time was that this would become another defining moment in my life.

I sat in the bleachers, and one by one, affluent speakers from all walks of life stepped onstage, and each speaker was introduced as earning 1 million dollars or more. I thought that was impossible. How could it be? This was the year 2000 and one million dollars seemed like an unattainable amount of money.

This was starting to catch my attention. At one point, a female speaker walked onstage. She was blonde, in her 40s, very professional. She was introduced as yet another 1-million-dollar earner. Her presentation focused on money, but she also discussed quantum physics, and how the money was "energy" and we needed to learn how to view money differently. While listening to her, I knew I wanted to be like her. I wanted to be a blonde, professional woman who earns one million dollars per year, standing onstage and influencing large groups of people.

I didn't want to be me anymore. I essentially made a decision that I would no longer be a 22-year-old party girl going nowhere in life and living in never-ending debt.

The following day, I walked around the convention hall, and I noticed many large financial institutions were at this event. Everything hit me at once, and I realized there was no way this was a scam if all these major corporations were here. And on top of that, what if all these speakers were sincere? What if I too could earn as much money as they did? That was the moment I finally decided to commit myself 100% to this business.

I spent the next six months pursuing my license. In January 2001, I officially earned that license. And within a year, I was promoted to Senior Marketing Director. I spent a lot of time working on building a team and learning the basics, and I had continuous mentorship. Everyone was mission-based and it was a very rewarding experience; more than mortgage/real estate could have ever been.

Things have not always been easy, but I always felt I was part of something larger than myself. As I worked, it became less about the money we were earning and more about our mission to help change lives and free people from debt and financial struggles.

I love what we stand for, and this business has become a very important part of my life. They say that when you are serving people, you are happiest. And I have to say that statement is 100% true.

I always knew at some point I would want to start a family. But I wanted a business that would give me the ability to stay home when I needed to while providing me with that *residual income* John Shin mentioned all those years ago. Fortunately, I found that here.

I spent the first ten years in business laying a good foundation with many sharp ups and downs. I found some great business partners over those years, and we went on some unbelievable vacations with the company. My second ten years were very different. I ended up meeting my husband David Horenstein in 2006, and we married in 2008, about a month before the entire country went into a deep recession.

David worked in real estate development. Following the recession, that all but halted. Because there was no real opportunity in real estate development at that time, he decided to join me in my business. We had our daughter Shayna in 2009 and our son Ely in 2012. I'm so glad that I spent those first ten years building that foundation, so when the babies came, I was able to be a mom and still run my business.

David has a completely different skill set than I do, and he was able to look at what we did with a different set of eyes. We worked very hard as a "power couple," and together we climbed the ranks of the company. Working together as a married couple can be very challenging, but those challenges will help you grow. With David's help, we were able to come up with a detailed plan for success, implement fully our business format system designed by WFG, but not always followed precisely. Together we ran an office and did our best to inspire everyone who chose to work with us.

There are a few things I've learned along the way that I personally feel are the keys to success. I have a couple pearls of wisdom I'd like to share in the hopes that they will help and inspire you, as they have me.

Tips for Success

#1: Mentors

I cannot stress this enough. Mentors are vital to your success! You need someone to teach you, someone you can learn from and someone you can aspire to become. I'm eternally grateful to Jamie and Shawn Villalovos for introducing me to this path and coaching me continuously through good times and bad. Also to John and Arlene Shin who not only trained me when I was a rookie but also welcomed me into their home as family. Both couples have served as incredible examples of success not only in business, but as a family. I also give credit to a business coach by the name of Sam Lin, who helped me tremendously in my early days. This coaching was invaluable.

Other mentors that have shaped who I am as a person today, and have provided incredible support and direction as well as becoming great friends are: Dan and Sophia Charlier; Ed and Kristianna Mylett; Bill and Peggy Mitchell; Jeff and

Cam Levitan; Greg and Tina Kapp; Rich and Cindy Thawley; Monte and Lisa Holm; Elan and Dina Michael; Rob and Tiffany Day and countless others: Thank you all for helping me shape my mindset and inspire me to become the best possible businesswoman I could be. Thank you for inspiring me. I believe that it is very important to take counsel from people that are either where you want to be or are heading in the direction you are heading. I can look back to so many defining moments coming through adversity, and me asking the right questions to the right people that led me to where I am today.

#2: Learning Success Principles

Before I earned my license, I was encouraged to read books like *Rich Dad Poor Dad*, *Think and Grow Rich*, *How to Win Friends and Influence People*, as well as *177 Mental Toughness Secrets of the World Class*. I truly believe in order to win in the business world, it is not enough to show up, and it's not enough to work hard. You must apply the winning success principles to your own life. You must have a burning desire. You must know *why* you are going into your business, and you must strive for that success. I had an opportunity to visit the NFL hall of fame this year due to our relationship with Marshall Faulk. We had a chance to study why so many people start playing sports, or start a business, and why so few succeed. You can draw a definite conclusion that the principles that it takes to go from someone playing sports casually and for fun to someone that has it in their mind to become number one and have a shot at being in the hall of fame mirror those principles that it takes to make it to the hall of fame of business and life.

#3: Faith

Life will get rough, and you will encounter many ob-stacles, but you must have faith. Faith will be there for you when you're scared, when adversity hits, and when you're not even sure you believe in yourself anymore. Your faith must be rock-solid. When you are at your darkest moments and you begin to question why things are happening to you, it is prayer and your faith that will keep you moving forward. Belief that God's plan intends for you to be where you are today because it is that path, and continuing to move forward on it, is the way to reach the destination you are meant to reach.

#4: Be Around People That Believe in You

I was told by people like Jaime, Dan, and Ed that they believed in me. I remember Rich Thawley telling me that he saw me at the top of the company someday. I will also never forget, at one of my darkest moments, receiving a phone call from Jaime telling me that I would be *#1* in our company. She told me stories of every successful person, including herself, hitting their highest peaks shortly after being hit the hardest. These little things matter, and you may change the course of someone's life by simply telling someone he or she has what it takes to succeed.

#5: Clearly Defined Goals and a Business Plan

You cannot win at the highest levels without having goals *and* a complete business plan written down. You need to read it daily and update it every year. If your plan doesn't get you excited, it probably isn't defined enough. You need to add fire to it; and it, in turn, needs to fire you up. I remember for years, I felt that this advice was nonsense and all I needed to do was work hard. It was many years into the business that I was challenged by Jaime to write a detailed plan. I only did it out of obligation. I wrote down huge goals and fantasies of a life I wanted to live. Part of me didn't truly believe I could achieve these things. Still, I wrote it down, read it daily, and said my affirmations every morning. 10 years later, I found that first plan I had written out. To my absolute surprise, I realized I had achieved almost everything I written down, to the very fine details. So much so that the first business plan seemed almost prophetic. I realized that having a written plan was not an option, it is an absolute must.

#6: Giving Back

100% of what we earn belongs to God, but his command is that he gets the first 10%. This is the only law in the Bible in which he says, "Test me." I have been giving 10% since first learning this, and I believe it is the key to long-term success and happiness. Part of my original business plan was to be part of Jeff Levitans *All for One* foundation. I remember seeing videos of all the children being helped and the great work they do. I remember being so honored when I was asked to join the board and be part of helping children in need. In addition to this, we give to many causes important to us, including our temple, Chabad of the Conejo Valley, and the anti-defamation league. It feels absolutely great to be able to help while also follow God's plan for tithing.

#7: Hard Work

I know, this kind of goes without saying, doesn't it? But so many people believe they can succeed without trying very hard. I do not believe that anything worthwhile is easy. Whether it's raising kids, running a business, or staying in shape, it requires hard work, counseling, and lots of discipline. I believe if you want to play in the big leagues, you can't treat this like a hobby. You need to treat it as if you're an athlete trying to be #1.

#8: Patience

I have watched great leaders struggle financially before their incomes caught up with their work ethic. I believe if you are doing the right things and you have great mentors in your corner, you need to keep going. They say an overnight success takes 10-15 years to manifest.

#9: Personal Growth

I am currently reading *The Laws of Success* by Napoleon Hill. In life, you are either growing or dying. You must always be growing, learning, and working to become a better, stronger version of yourself. If you find yourself stuck in the same place you were five years ago, you aren't growing and you haven't reached your full potential. I have invested hundreds of thousands of dollars in my personal growth. If you are afraid to spend money on yourself to grow, it becomes very hard to become the version of yourself that you want to become. Athletes have coaches, many business icons have worked with coaches, and I believe that it is important to constantly upgrade yourself to the next level. I joined Ed Mylett and Andy Frisella's Arete Syndicate when he launched that because I knew I needed to grow past where I was at the time.

#10: Don't Give Up!

When you are in business for yourself, you can never quit. Quitting means you have given up on yourself. Wherever you go, there you are. If you are doing something that you know can change your life, but you quit saying "it's not for me" or it's not my passion, I know from experience this is usually an excuse. If you take that same mentality into the next thing you try, you will experience similar results. It's better to analyze why you started in the first place, re write your business plan, get a mentor that is in your business and succeeding, and then work hard towards your goals. You will find that success is usually three feet from where you are when you had the idea of quitting. (Taken from Three feet from Gold by Sharon Lechter). I also believe that the people you take counsel from at your quitting moments is everything. So many times I was feeling down and out, and my phone would almost always ring. It would be my great mentor and friend Dan Charlier. I can recall a conversation where I told him I was done. I had written out a resignation letter and was starting to make other plans. He invited me over that night and said to me, "quitters never win, and winners never quit". He told me to buckle down and get back to work. I am forever grateful for his words and encouragement. What if I had gotten counsel from someone who was a quitter in their own life?

My vision for the future is that Virtuity becomes the official brand for athletes to affiliate with after they retire from sports. Virtuity is also a place for women entrepreneurs to shine. It is a place for men and women to build businesses with massive passive income. And finally, it is a place for families to build a business together.

I also see Virtuity as a place for professionals like CPAs, attorneys, realtors and mortgage brokers to affiliate themselves.

I am beyond thankful for my team, our top leaders featured in this book, as well as our mentors. Without the tireless efforts of our team, Virtuity would not exist.

I am thankful for my family, who have always supported me as I've worked to build my business. I truly believe this is just the beginning and there are many more years of hard work and success to come.

Hanna L. Horenstein, (818) 402-9396, hlhorenstein@aol.com

RUDY LASRY

I am from a family of immigrants. I have two siblings.

My parents were born in Morocco and migrated to Israel when they were young children. In 1989 my parents moved from Israel to the United States. They left government and union jobs in Israel. When my family immigrated, my father studied for his contractor's license. Once he completed the testing and gained his license, my father became a general contractor in the United States.

This was a big change for the Lasry family. In Israel, my parents had jobs with benefits and guarantees. They came home early at very predictable times. They were always available to my siblings and me.

I lived in a tiny town about thirty minutes away from the Dead Sea. In a small town, everyone tends to know one another. And that was the case in our town called Dimona. Children played in the streets daily, and the environment was warm and safe.

When we immigrated to the United States, everything changed. The cities here were enormous in size. Our neighbors really did not interact with one another. And playing in the street was not very safe. This limited us to playing in our fenced backyard.

In addition to this change, everyone in the family had to learn English.

At some point in time, my parents started in entrepreneurship. This endeavor required hard work, long hours and complete dedication.

Life changed from our regular dinners together to one of aloneness for us children. There had always been the comfort of coming home to our parents after school. Now we had to learn that our parents would not be around and available. We had big financial struggles in the beginning.

In the early 1990's, my parents came close to losing our home. The housing market crashed and construction work was scarce in California. This era was after a major Northridge earthquake.

It took my parents about ten years, into the early 2000's, to get into a more comfortable place. It took the same timeframe to become financially comfortable and become established in the United States. Once they were established, they started to thrive.

My parent's example of migrating to the USA in their mid-thirties; taking such a big risk and leaving government/union jobs for a greater call; and becoming entrepreneurs was the example that led me down the path of entrepreneurship. They showed me that working hard for a better life, a life filled with freedom and possibilities, is more rewarding and exciting than working a job.

However, I did not realize this until I was about twenty-four years of age. I found myself done with college and stuck working in the restaurant industry. I was employed as a waiter and a bartender. I quickly became fed up with being paid low wages. I was in debt and prayed for some kind of an answer and a different life.

At the age of twenty-four, I was carrying more than thirty thousand dollars in debt. No one had ever educated me about money. And at this point in his life, no one was willing to educate me either. The financial industry seemed more interested in keeping me ignorant and in debt than helping me get out of debt.

When I was eighteen years old and on the first day on my college campus, I was introduced to credit card companies. They seemed really attractive initially, offering giveaways such as T-shirts, clocks and gimmicky things, I just had to have all those "free" giveaways. So, I signed up for several cards and several weeks later they showed up in the mail.

In the mid 1990's, I received a call from my buddies about attending a Pearl Jam concert in San Jose, California. It seemed like a fun trip, but I did not have the funds. It was at that point that I realized I had received a credit card. When I opened it, the limit was $2,000! $2,000?? I could not believe it. For an eighteen-year-old kid in 1995 that felt like $100,000 and that I could never spend that much.

Well, fast forward just a few years and that became a way of life of spending more than what you earn. Buy it now, because you want it now. I even traded my perfectly paid off car (1988 300zx Nissan) and got myself into a car loan, in which I was paying three hundred dollars a month. This was just about the time where cars added controls to the steering wheel. And I just thought it was so cool and had to have it.

By age twenty-four. I owed nineteen thousand dollars on a car loan and fifteen thousand dollars on credit cards. I was considering moving back in with mom and dad to save money on rent and bills. I could no longer afford to support myself on a waiter's wage of roughly $2,000 per month.

I developed my people skills in the restaurant industry and learned how to connect with people. I always took pride in my vocation. I felt like I was a natural-born and passionate entrepreneur but had no idea of how to pursue anything. I had given a shot at a business degree but was discouraged to find that my business teacher had never owned a business.

I had a dream, for a brief moment, at possibly becoming a dentist. But when I learned of the high cost of dental school and the dedication required, I chose not to go that route.

In January of 2002, I met Hanna Horenstein in the Holly-wood Hills, at my friend's party. Hanna changed the trajectory of my life and introduced me to the financial services industry. Hanna educated me about simple concepts that most people don't know or understand because of their seeming complexity.

I learned of the importance of budgeting, paying off debt, the high cost of waiting to invest, how taxes and investments work and my favorite *"the rule of 72"* realized by Albert Einstein. I was able to apply these simple concepts right away and get on track financially. I saw hope and believed that things would be good. I was now on a simple path to pay off my debt in five years and was hopeful.

Prior to meeting Hanna, the goal was to move back in with Mom and Dad; and that scared me tremendously. At that age, my biggest concern about living with mom and dad was what do you do at the end of a date night? Immature thinking, but nonetheless, the thinking of a twenty-four-year old boy.

Hanna, at the same time, was helping me understand and take a hold of my financial life. She was helping me change the relationship that I had with money. She asked me if I would like to learn how to not just manage my money better, but would I like to learn how to change the relationship with how I earned money as well. I was intrigued and considered working with Hanna part-time. I wanted to learn how to become a business owner in financial services.

I accepted the challenge and saw tremendous potential in working with someone as dedicated and successful as Hanna was and is today. I began working in the financial services industry part-time. Initially I had a very challenging time getting the appropriate licenses, due to a marijuana offense that I had on my record when I was eighteen years old. What is unfortunate is that today the offense that I had is legal.

I considered quitting, because without my licenses, I was limited. I would not be able to become an advisor, help people, or earn an income. Hanna saw much potential and dedication in me, so she had me start off by running the mortgage branch at our office. I was responsible for something that I had never done before. But very quickly, I learned and helped develop that part of the business.

I started realizing great success throughout the state of California. I was able to quit my waiter job within six months of working with Hanna. I paid off all my debt within those six months and had some substantial savings. I soon became a mentor to a number of business associates and started building a financial company of my own with *WFG's* opportunity and system.

I was introduced to a movement disguised as a company; it has changed my life. I initially ran a very successful mortgage branch with Hanna and developed my financial agency. In my second year of business, Hanna & I opened our own office and I achieved a six-figure income.

The years prior, I had never earned more than thirty thousand dollars per year, so this was a life change in a very positive direction. After four years of pleading my case and fighting, I began to earn my advisor license designation. Eventually getting fully licensed and even being responsible for a securities branch. I became the branch manager. I was told by many regulators, that I would most likely not ever get my securities licenses; they were all wrong!

Hanna and I ran a branch together for close to six years and had many ups and downs. The good times, where we became accustomed to expensive daily lunches, company trips and two really young kids, running, romping, and doing as they want. The low times were very difficult and riddled with leadership issues and personal challenges which eventually lead to our moving out of the office and opening our own individual offices.

I left the office with Hanna with close to eighty thousand dollars in debt. It felt like the money was always going to come and this was the end of 2007. The economy was going through a huge downturn, mortgages dried up and it was time for change and a makeover. Initially, this seemed devastating but at this time I met Amanda, my soon to be wife. My goals and whys in life started to develop and grow and the true purpose appeared. My purpose was to be a husband, a family man, a devoted believer in God and doing great things in the world.

Amanda and I met on a sailing trip to Catalina. My brother, Alzy and my sister in-law Julie, were the ones who put the trip together. Initially I was not interested in attending the trip and Amanda was initially not invited. Someone dropped off the list of attendees. Amanda was invited and I, at the last minute, was forced by my brother to attend. So, I did.

It was one of the most magical moments in my life when I met Amanda by the sailboat. Amanda was there with a friend (boy) who, she was somewhat friendly with. When I met her, I just had this amazing feeling and the best way to describe it was LOVE AT FIRST SITE! After shaking Amanda's hand, my brother and I went to park the car. Before boarding the boat, all I had on my mind was how wonderful Amanda was.

On the boat, Amanda was a bit standoffish and I had to find a way to get her attention. So, I befriended all the other women on the boat. There were a total of fourteen passengers and four of them were single women.

I felt I had to make a connection with someone for Amanda to notice me. So, I did make a connection with one of the single women, Ericka. What do you know? Amanda started to notice me.

We started chatting about exercise and food and anything else we could. That evening we arrived at Catalina. We all went out to a Mexican restaurant, where I cozied up to Amanda. I asked for her telephone number. I made my intentions clear, and that I enjoyed her company.

There was one issue. Tim! (the boy who was friendly with Amanda). The next morning the women went on a "women walk" and the men did the same thing, separately. This was my opportunity to get to know Tim. I wanted to find out what Tim's relationship and intentions with Amanda were. Tim said "well Amanda could be a candidate" with snobbishly demeanor. This is all I needed to hear, in order to pursue my goal of making a deeper connection with Amanda.

That evening the entire crew had a white dressed party on the boat with food, drinks, and music. This was the evening where I solidified things with Amanda. We ate together, swam together, drank together and towards the end of the evening did the dishes together while dancing and connected on a deep level.

I was head over heels in love!! When I invited Amanda to kiss me, she did, and the rest was history. When we parted the boat that Sunday, I reached out to Amanda. I insisted that I did not want to wait or play a game. I wanted to see her right away and that Wednesday, which was the 4th of July, we had our first ten-hour date. Following the Sunday date, we spent twenty-four hours together.

Following a trip to Santa Barbara, I never left her side

from that time forward. Within five months, we moved in together. Two years and nineteen days later, from the day we met, we married. The following year, we had our first daughter and every two years after, we had three more daughters for a total of four. I was living my dream as a devoted husband, father, and businessman all under God's covenant.

In business, I enjoy helping people, educating them in regard to myths they have about money and how money works. I believe that success is not measured by how much money you earn or attain, however lack of money brings frustration & misery.

When Amanda and I moved in together, we created a plan to pay off the eighty thousand dollars in debt that I had. Amanda and I were able to pay off this debt within just over a year.

The following year after, we were able to save our first six figures and that was just the beginning. Amanda's and my success in business grew. We developed people and mentored them and showed them how they can also build a business. Amanda and I have developed six figure income earners and multiple six figure income earners and have a passion to paying this knowledge forward.

I understand that the lack of money does not allow you to be who you're supposed to be on this earth. While money can be a measure of success, true success is how many people you've served in your life and the example you set daily.

In business my passion is twofold:

The first passion is to show people that they can become entrepreneurs, achieve what they truly desire in life and win at high levels. Get people to dream again.

The second passion is to reach countless families and educate them on how money works, on the importance of being debt free, protecting the worst-case scenario (death & disability) & the importance of savings & investing for the present and future.

On a personal note, I love spending time with my beautiful wife, Amanda and our four girls. Our family are avid skiers and snowboarders. We constantly travel to Mammoth Mountain in the eastern Sierras, Utah Canyons, Sun Valley, Telluride Colorado and many other mountain locations. We also enjoy the beaches of the world such as Balboa Island, Hawaii, Caribbean, Croatia, Venice and many more.

In 2018 our family decided to leave Los Angeles and explore other places to live in the United States. We fell in love with Colorado, the colorful state. We expanded our business over to the Denver Tech Center and now live in a peaceful gated community on a golf course. Amanda's and my dream of our kids being able to run around on the streets, climb trees, know all their neighbors and have a small town feel finally came true. I was desperate to give my kids a taste of the way I grew up. Amanda & I truly found the community we prayed for.

On a separate note being such an avid snowboarder, I now live ninety minutes away from Keystone and Breckenridge. I am two hours away from world renowned resorts like Vail, which is truly a dream come true for me. All of my girls love to ski. Even Amanda is developing a slow passion for it. Amanda's big passion is being a beach girl and wearing flip flops 365 days a year.

Rudy Lasry, (818) 599-1485,
Rudy_lasry@yahoo.com
Amanda Lasry, Amanda_lasry@yahoo.com

GENE COPPA

The Beginning:

Los Angeles, CA in the 1970s. The days of smog alerts, *Star Wars*, the Dodgers, and inflation. I grew up in a middle-class family in East L.A. My father worked as an accountant. My mother was a stay-at-home-mom. There were 4 of us kids growing up in the house. Our family possessed a strong work ethic and a deep commitment to religion. Until I was in fifth grade, I thought I was going to be a priest. And then I noticed girls.

I always had an entrepreneurial streak. At five years old, I already started my own business: I dragged my little red wagon around and collected my neighbors' newspapers. I put them in brown grocery bags and loaded them into my mom's station wagon where we would take them to the recycling center, otherwise known as the dump.

In high school, I was building computers for people while being involved in numerous activities. I started my first "official job" at 14, before I was legally allowed a work permit. In college, I commuted from the West Side at UCLA to downtown Los Angeles by bus. I did this several days a week in order to network and do computer consulting for local businesses. I did that until I got a job with the UCLA Police Department as a campus security escort. That job changed the direction of my life.

After working only a couple of months for the police department, they promoted me to dispatcher. After that, I decided I was going to become a police officer. After graduating from UCLA, I was hired as an officer for the city of Santa Barbara.

I had found my calling, my duty. I loved every minute of the job. From bicycle patrol to narcotics work, to pulling over drunk drivers, to helping little old ladies cross the street; from car chases and tangling with bad guys, I knew I was going to be a police officer forever. Until I wasn't.

Three years into my career, I hurt my back in a fight with a suspect. My law enforcement career ended instantly. I went through years of physical therapy and multiple "non-surgical" procedures. I saw doctors, surgeons, and chiropractors. I never went back to work as a police officer.

Depressed, bitter, and furious with the world, I looked at my newborn baby girl, and I decided to pursue a career in law *practice*, rather than enforcement. From 1999-2000, while I was applying for law school, I began working as a mortgage broker. I later turned that side hustle into a mortgage company.

I started law school in 2001 at UCLA, all while running my own mortgage business. After 3 years of doing those side-by-side, buying and selling two houses, having another baby girl, and generally living a busy life, I was recruited into one of the largest law firms in the country. Over the course of the next seven years, I moved from that firm to another, continued to run my mortgage company, and tried to maintain a personal life at the same time. It was lucrative, I was making a lot of money, but no matter how much money I earned, it wasn't about the money; the job wasn't fulfilling me.

I did everything I could to spend a lot of time with my family, which was nearly impossible with the legal career I chose. But I found ways to do it. I was at every one of my daughters' events. I coached their sports and went to their recitals and competitions (they are amazing dancers). I made myself available as much as possible to be part of their lives.

On February 14, 2007, I purchased a mortgage company from a pastor/retired cop. I planned to add that company to my existing mortgage business, but it turned out nothing he told me about the business was true, and he had falsified his records. While it was economically painful, it turned out to be a good learning experience for me. This happened about six months before the mortgage meltdown and one of the worst economic downturns in US history. The mortgage business suffered dramatically. And I had just bought a million-dollar home with a huge mortgage. I relied on the income from my legal career to support us, but the pay was not even close to enough. We lived off my income and the "equity" in our house.

In 2010, after seven years at the two firms, the great recession, and the mortgage meltdown, I decided it was time to leave the big firm life and start my own law firm. I needed the independence. I needed to be meaningful. I needed to be the master of my own future. I continued to run my mortgage company, but it wasn't doing well. Fortunately, since my new law practice was booming, I could sustain the company. However, as the industry I practiced law in went downhill, it was amazing how many clients decided not to pay their bills, or they decided they didn't want to pay as much as they had agreed to in the first place.

Introduction to the Business:

In 2011, I received a call from someone from WFG, someone who wanted to arrange a meeting with me. I booked that meeting and ended up being introduced to Hanna Horenstein. After that initial meeting, she called me periodically over the next four months trying to arrange a follow-up meeting. Each time she called, I told her "not now" or "I'm really busy" or any number of different excuses in order to avoid meeting with her again.

But she was persistent, and I finally agreed to meet with her again. I agreed to get involved in a "referral" type of partnership where each of us referred clients to the other in order to help the clients and create additional business. I was very skeptical about every aspect of the business: its structure, the people involved, why everyone was so happy and excited all the time, how people made money, why it looked so different from all the other companies, etc.

Part of getting involved also resulted in me looking over my own financial picture. I had always been pretty well-insured, as far as life insurance is concerned. But because of my introduction to WFG, I decided to get some additional insurance that would never end, permanent insurance. I am very glad I did because in 2012, I blacked out while driving, and I drove straight into a wall at fifty miles per hour. I broke my neck, ended up in emergency surgery and later, the doctors told me I crashed because I had developed epilepsy. Had it not been for the life insurance policies I had taken out, I would not have been able to get the insurance that my family and I needed. After I recovered, I knew I wanted to help others understand their own personal risks so they could take care of their families also.

Once I started getting heavily involved in the business, I realized I was not very good at listening to instructions. I always tried to find a better, more efficient way of doing things. I was not coachable. During this time, I also had a number of things happening in my personal life that were causing me to lose focus on the business. Then I hit a low point in my life, personally, professionally, and spiritually.

It wasn't until that low point, though, that I started to regain some clarity. I put my faith back where it should have been all along: God. I was rediscovering my faith in God, and I saw that I had only two options in life: I could give up or I could continue to fight. God had already told me that giving up wasn't an option, so I began to rebuild my life. I wanted to create a life I could be proud of. And I did. It took a lot of time and hard work, but I did it. And it would not have happened without God leading me to WFG where I learned the success principles that helped me flourish.

For the first 5 years in the business, I was "involved" but mainly looking for reasons why the business wasn't "legit." At year 5, I finally realized that everything I had been looking at was really the greatest platform I have ever seen to allow individuals the opportunity to change their lives and reach the dreams they have. While there's no guarantee (there never is), you don't get that opportunity very many places. Once I figured this out, I still was in a place in my life that I could pursue it.

It wasn't until my eighth year in the business that I finally passed my $100,000 mark in cashflow. For me, that $100,000 mark was merely a stepping stone, not an end goal. It proved to me that no matter who you are, you can reach for your own achievements.

When it comes to success, there is no substitute for hard work. However, hard work in and of itself does not automatically guarantee success. I've worked very hard in school, many jobs and several entrepreneurial efforts. I was successful in some, and unsuccessful in others, despite the fact that I worked hard in all of them.

The key to my success, so far, has been changing my focus onto the success principles. While I have always been a very positive and happy person, my old habits of concern, over-thinking, skepticism, disbelief, personal guilt, self-doubt, and fear of failure have caused me the most stagnation. They did not help me grow, and they definitely did not help me succeed.

When I replaced those failed principles with coachability,

action, definiteness of purpose, belief in myself and focus, my life began to change drastically. This change allowed more room in my life for happiness, gratitude and positivity, which in turn lead to more coachability, action, definiteness of purpose, belief in myself, focus, etc., and the cycle continues.

Throughout my life, the one key for success I have always lived by is the belief and ability to handle any adversity. I have gone through more adversity than I care to discuss, and I have found, as Ed Mylett says, that the adversities in my life have happened FOR me not TO me. I take each obstacle head-on, and I look for all the ways that challenge will help me grow and improve. Adaptability and gratitude for your present and your future make hard-work and tenacity turn to success.

I've always loved the poem "Footprints" in which a man walks with God along a beach. The beach represents the course of his life, and during the majority of that life, he sees two sets of footprints in the sand: one belonging to him and another belonging to God. But he notices that during the most difficult times, he only sees one set of footprints in the sand. The man questions God, asking why, during those saddest and most troublesome times, God abandoned him and made him walk alone.

God simply replied, "My son, I love you, and I would never leave you. During your times of suffering, when you could only see one set of footprints, it was then that I carried you."

It is through focus, definiteness of purpose, action, coachability, gratitude and belief in myself that my future is bright. But it's only bright because I have made the decisions to treat people right and to always do what is in their best interests. Whether that person or family is an associate, a referral, or someone we met on the street for the first time a few minutes ago, it is our duty to do everything within our power to help them. Focus on others, including the development of those on my team and in my life, creates and solidifies my vision of the future.

By focusing on doing the right thing for others, I am confident that when those times arise, and they always will, of difficulty, pain and doubt, there will only be one set of footprints in the sand; and it won't be mine.

Gene Coppa, (805) 701-7012,
gacoppa@gmail.com

GRANT WRIGHT

"Grant, how are we going to eat?" Emily said.

"I have no idea." I said.

"What do we have?" Emily said.

"There is a gift card that I won from phone zone that we can use," I responded

"What can we get with that $5 gift card?" Emily asked.

"If I add a couple of dollars, we can get some hot food options they offer. It can hold us over until our check hits for work," I said.

"Ok fine." Emily accepted.

That's how my career with *Virtuity* started. I'm not saying this is the ideal way. I have seen people start with a much better foundation. They were married, owned a home, income, savings, the whole MACHO set up. But you never know who the champion is until they get hit! That's what sets apart a champion vs a loser.

Hanna always said, "it's not about how hard you hit but how hard you can get hit and still keep going." All the people that gives the people in this book the Virtuity edge is because we are led by some of the most mentally tough people with David and Hanna Horenstein.

Adversity hits everyone. But with the Horensteins, they fall down, dust themselves off, then come back stronger. When you have that example, what else can you do but rise to the occasion and get better.

My story started at my kitchen table, which was really a card table with mismatched chairs. David Horenstein and Vicky, who was Emily's sisters' friend, did a field training. They wanted to teach us some basic concepts on how money works and see if I can send some referrals. I was very reluctant on taking the meeting because I was so "busy."

They persisted and once they sat down and showed the power of what they do, I was immediately sold within the first 10 minutes. I figured "how often do you have successful people walk into your house, teach about how they got successful, and be willing to mentor you until you are successful?" I asked, "can I do this?"

He said, "come by the office and check it out first."

He wanted to make sure that I was a good fit. I showed up to the Westlake office on March 1st. I walked in and music was playing. There were friendly people in suits, and for a guy like me, I was at home. People were nicer than most people that I had been around.

I went with David into the business overview where he went over everything. He showed me what Virtuity does and why they do what they do. I was thinking that if I can do this, it would be game changing. This was exactly what I was looking for.

They were going to:

• Bring me on board • Train me • Coach me • Mentor me • Teach me • Encourage me • Praise me • Recognize me, and possibly • Transform my whole life

That promise was met and yet is still just getting started. When I got started, it was not the story I was confident that it was going to be. I knew I wanted to be successful, and I knew that I had what it takes. But what I soon realized was that I wasn't the person that could bring on the success that I wanted.

I was a student in personal development. I attended so many seminars, had read a lot of personal development books, and I thought it was because I had read them that I was going to be successful.

A lot of those books miss very important parts that are necessary to win in anything. "Are you the type of person when no one is watching that is successful?" What you do when no one is watching has a lot more to do with your success than anything else.

It was December of 2014, and the team and I were "running" for SMD. When I say running, I was in the office, the team was on vacation. Hanna was in the office and she just got off the phone with David.

She came to where I was and was explaining the difference

between those who are succeeding and those who aren't. We all have the same opportunities. What makes someone make fifty thousand dollars in December and another person who goes into debt in December? She asked what are they focusing on and what am I focusing on? One person is focusing on buying stuff that they can't afford. Hanna was focusing on helping more people and making money because of it.

That actually left a huge imprint on me. I started to see success was not so much that some people are successful and some people are not. Success is not some luck of the draw. I found that it has a lot to do with mentality. Poor mentality hates work. Rich mentality values work.

Poor mentality makes money, spends money, borrows money, and spends more money. Rich mentality makes money, keeps money, and grows money, until they are financially free.

Poor mentality hopes everything is going to work out while rich mentality does everything they can to make sure it does work out.

They control as many controllable as they can. These are just some of the lessons I have learned being in an office of David and Hanna Horenstein.

THE MOMENT OF TRUTH

I was getting really good at getting some amazing information that I knew would eventually change my life. Of course, once I applied it. But I wasn't applying everything that I learned. How much longer was I going to be a spectator or a player in this game called life? There are people wanting to see how much they can push the envelope. Those same people want to get out of their comfort zone and see what they can create. I saw people doing that all around me. But I never said, "it's time for me to bet on myself now!"

It started when I was at a big event. I was listening to Jeff Levitan speak. I was on the verge of doing what I do best. QUITTING!

Everything I had ever started I had quit.

Just a short list: ● Basketball ● Football ● Track ● College ● Business major ● Film major ● Acting ● Stand up ● T-shirt business ● Screen printing business ● Marketing business ● Basketball camp and so much more!

So, while I was listening to Jeff Levitan, I was also rerunning all the times that I had quit. Things that I believe I could have been great at if I would have gone all in. Jeff Levitan says "force coming from the outside and life is over, but force coming from the inside, there's a new life coming."

I was realizing that it was not the pressure from the outside that was killing me. This is pressure in my heart. I want to be the best. I want to be successful. I'm tired of losing. I'm tired of not giving something my all. I'm tired of where my family and I are at! I know we can do more, be more, share more, create more. It's time to bet on myself! And that's what I kept on saying!

IT'S TIME TO BET ON MYSELF.

I went to my boss and told him that I quit. I went full-time with *Virtuity*. Eight months later I was a Senior Marketing Director with my own office. Once I went all in, success happened.

Whenever I drifted, **ZERO** success.

I floundered the first two and a half years. Some flounder ten years, others take immediate massive action as soon as they get there. The only difference is the moment that you make your decision. Since I went all in, I started building a team of my own. *THE DREAM CRUSADERS*

The one thing that I love, that *Virtuity* has taught me, is that I can build it how I want it. My faith is very important to me, and they've always encouraged me to strengthen my faith. *Dream Crusaders* is a team on the move to be a Force for Good. We want to think of ourselves as God's hands and feet. We have sat down with numerous people that said, "I was praying for something like this."

As a matter of fact, I prayed for something like this. I am so grateful that we live in a country that supports free enterprise. It supports the person who is willing to bring a better product to the customer or client. They have an opportunity to do good for their family. I love how the company that has the best products and best marketing wins.

I know *Virtuity* is the best company around. I was able to start a business with **No employees, No overhead, No payroll, No inventory, No workers comp, No cold calling, No door to door, No boss, No politics, No quotas, No territory restrictions, No time clock**

Unlimited income, potential residual income, passive income, paid twice a week bonus income, multimillion dollar mentor ship, faith and family focused, non-captive world class recognition, world class events, world class trips, world class financial education, world class leadership, and examples of success. And you can do it! You don't have to wait for someone to like you, no experience needed, we train people from A to Z.

And we are constantly getting better every day. You can do this part-time, full-time, all the time or spare time! Most people are employees. And when you are an employee, there are natural challenges that immediately arise. The first is not making enough money. The reason is because the employer pays the position and not the person. So, if you are a person that wants to do the best, help the company grow and be a valuable asset most of the time you are still going to get paid twenty-five dollars per hour.

So, what ends up happening is the employee gets tired of that and look for a second job. This is when the frustration really starts to build. Now you have a second job and no time. You are working just to work. So, naturally you start looking for a higher paying job. You find out there are not a lot out there.

So, for some, they just give up and shrink their goals to fit with the income they are making at that time. But the other person says I have to figure something else out. They get into real estate, phlebotomy, hair, etc. It cost them thousands of dollars and a lot of time, if not tens of thousands and a lot of time to get started with any of those.

What if there was a way to make a couple extra hundred if not thousands without having to spend all that time trading time for money? This is how *Virtuity* started becoming the best company in the industry. We innovated the way business is done. We revolutionized the way work was done. We asked different question. We asked better questions.

How can we give the people that need some extra income a better opportunity out there? How can we give the people that want to be in management a better opportunity and allow them to make more money as they help the company to grow? How can we give the person in sales a better opportunity with building a team and passive residual income? How can we give the recruiters a better opportunity? How can we give the investor a better opportunity? How can we give the entrepreneur a better opportunity?

We didn't stop at one. We want to change the way business is done! We are just getting started, and we are going to see *Virtuity* in magazines, documentaries, books… oh too late. We did not come here to take part we came here to take over!

Dream Crusaders is a team within *Virtuity* who will have one thousand licensed agents in five years, with thirty SMDs, multiple six and seven figure earners. Make the rest of your life the best of your life!

Grant Wright, (805) 298-3506,
wrightgrantw@yahoo.com

JOSEPH GOPEZ

At an early age, I learned the value of a dollar. Like many of you, I did not come from a wealthy family, and we struggled financially. This opened the door for negative energy like fear, feelings of unworthiness, and ultimately, a scarcity mindset. My main goal wasn't live, but to simply survive. I didn't ask for anything other than the bare minimum because my family couldn't afford anything extra. I learned not to dream big, because I knew those dreams would never come true.

Despite all my negative thinking, I did pretty well in school. My parents valued education, a degree, and a well-paying, stable job. After high school, I pursued a computer engineering degree at UC Irvine. It was supposed to be a five-year program, but I finished it in four years by taking summer school every year and adding an extra class to my schedule every semester. I wanted to get into the workforce and make money already! Also, I also didn't want to add another year of student loan debt. When I finally graduated, I did so during one of the biggest recessions in US history.

Thanks to my degree, I was able to find a job, and I earned a higher starting salary than most of my peers. I began advancing quickly, but something felt off. Like many people, I often daydreamed of retiring. I fantasized about all my upcoming vacations, the weekend, even the next lunch break. I didn't love my job. I was grateful I had one, and it did pay the bills, but it didn't offer me very much financial freedom, especially if I wanted to get married and start a family. Not only that, but it wasn't fulfilling, and it definitely wasn't something I wanted to do for the next forty years.

Around this time, a friend and coworker of mine suggested that I attend an open house with her. She had just started a part-time opportunity, and knowing I wanted to save more money, she wanted to share it with me. Needless to say, I had dozens of questions, and I bombarded her with all of them.

Her answers were somewhat vague, but the key points were: there is no cap on the income you make, you can start by working part-time, and you'll be working in the financial industry. It sounded too good to be true, so I repeatedly blew her off. But deep down, I was curious.

One day, I finally decided to go and just give it a try. That's when everything changed. I attended a meeting full of speakers and advisors who taught the basics of wealth. Even with a college education, there were several simple concepts I was hearing for the first time.

As I continued to learn, I had two realizations. One, I didn't want other families to experience financial hardship like mine did. And two: if I could teach this information to other struggling families and help them make money, it would be a win-win situation for everyone involved. So I dove in and interviewed with this firm.

I began meeting advisors in their offices, learning about the company's history, and listening to everyone's success stories. This firm was full of people like me, people who believed in saving money, having the right protections and insurance in place, as well as taking care of your family and helping others.

I found myself meeting people who made $500,000 a year, and they're unknowns in the company. I discovered there are literally hundreds of people making seven figures a year. The top person even made over $1,000,000 a month! It was incredible! Besides the massive amounts of income, these people had the most important resource of all: time.

They could take as much vacation time as they wanted and stay completely up to date on their bills. Many even choose to retire in their 20s or 30s. Many had great relationships with their spouses, complete with date night every week. The successful people here were incredible role models for their children that led by example rather than telling them what they *should* or *shouldn't* do.

I still had my suspicions about the firm, but I continued

going to the meetings. I commuted every morning through insane L.A. traffic. Friends thought I had lost my mind. Even I suspected I was a little crazy for doing this, but I just kept going.

To make matters worse, my background was in engineering, not finance. And honestly, I didn't have the greatest people skills. And for the cherry on top, I didn't even own a suit. But I was dedicated, and in my first year working with them, I made just over $40,000 part-time. By the way, I saved each and every penny of that money. Not only was I making money I never dreamed of as a child, but I was instructing other struggling families how they too could earn and save money.

I made a deal with myself: when I had accrued $100,000 in cash savings, I would fire my boss and open my own office back in the valley. That would bring me closer to my family. The next year, I did just that, and it was all because I committed to my goals.

You might have heard the phrase "If you don't believe, you won't receive." I find this to be true. Belief gives you incredible confidence that the job can get done. This provides the fuel necessary to achieve your goals. Without it, we tend to look for all the ways something can give up on our dreams.

Since starting my own company, my faith in God has grown immeasurably. I noticed that the more challenging my goal was, the more it required me to trust in God. Faith is an amazing and unlimited source of power. It's my first key to success.

There's a funny saying that goes: "If you want to make God laugh, tell him your plans." While I do believe you eventually get what you ask for, usually we don't get exactly what we think we want. There is an inevitable barrage of challenges and distractions that will test you throughout your journey. Having the perseverance to continue when you feel broken will carry you across the finish line.

I think this is why I turned into an endurance athlete junkie. I train and race in marathons, triathlons, ironmen's, etc... I choose to compete in this field for many reasons, and one of them is to improve my perseverance. These races are definitely grueling, but it is worth every bit of pain when I cross that finish line. Perseverance is my second key to success. And I've got goals that I'm actively working towards! I plan to run seven marathons on seven continents in seven days. On top of that, I also aim to successfully climb Mount Everest! When it comes to ambition, the sky is literally the limit, friends. It will take perseverance to run those marathons, just like it will take extreme perseverance to scale Mount Everest.

My third key to success is to continually work on improving yourself. I've spent tens of thousands of dollars on self-help books, I've attended self-development courses and business coaches to give myself a fighting chance to win. It's worth way more than the small price you invest. Developing is absolutely necessary. Set goals and work towards them. Never quit, never give in to defeat, and never stop learning, because life never stops teaching.

My family has been and always will continue to be the most important part of my life. I'm so grateful that I am able to be there for my family during the hard times, when they need me to be their rock. It's sweet that I can take time off without having to ask a manager for that time, but it's even sweeter not having to check my bank account and knowing that money will keep going in! The passive income that continues to snowball is a perk my old engineering job could never offer.

While achieving my own personal goals puts a big smile on my face, I am proud that I am able to live a life of service. I'm honored to play a role in others' success stories and help them get where they want to go; especially all the wonderful people on my team. Watching them grow, overcome challenges, and achieve their goals is one of the most rewarding feelings I've ever experienced.

Many of the core leaders are starting to step into their roles. They are taking major responsibility and are continually raising the bar for this team. There is no end in sight, and the only way is up. I'll see you at the top of the mountain.

Joseph Gopez, (818) 288-0918,
jpgopez@gmail.com

SARA ROSE MACIAS

Ever feel like you are the different one of the group?
Ever been shut down because you were way too excited?

Ever feel like the one in the family who has all of the dreams and goals? Then you can relate to me.

My name is Sara Rose Macias, but you may call me Rose. I come from a town called Colton, that is located in the San Bernardino County area of Southern California. My family and money never had a positive relationship. It has always been a taboo conversation for everyone as early as I can remember.

Culturally, my family grew up in a very Hispanic held household. Even though my father was my Mexican and Puerto Rican blood, my mother was known as the community "Guerra" of the family. She comes from Irish, Dutch, and German descent and cooked better Hispanic dishes than my father.

I wish I could say that my younger years were so exciting and stress free, but that was not the case. Those years define the persistence in me today. Managing money was never taught to me growing up. I know that I'm speaking to most when I say that. I remember my family always fighting about it, and it was never because we had too much of it.

"Comfortable getting by" was our motto, yet getting by was NEVER comfortable. I had two very educated parents with degrees. My father was a Respiratory Therapist and my mother a Recreational Therapist and Special Education Teacher. They did everything right and still found themselves laid off at those times when we needed income the most.

After their divorce, family illness hit. My father was diagnosed with Diabetes and the money issues worsened. That lead to the earnings all falling on my mom's back. Watching my mom clean rich people's houses is one of those times in my life that I will never forget. It was in one of those moments while watching what my mom had to do to get by that I made a promise to be the owner of the house, not the one cleaning it.

Years went by and I had to see my two brothers grow up mostly at dad's with me at mom's. Both of my brothers always made me feel like the odd one out. Abuse was present, but I constantly focused on the light.

I feel for split homes financially and mentally. Playing soccer was my therapy as a child. I was a goalie for years and had the nickname "Animal" that some would say could carry on today.

Only today, I'm an animal toward teaching financial literacy to everyone. Sports gave me a team, a family, and a sense that I was a part of something. If I wasn't the captain, I was doing what it took to be one. I was driven by winning and winning together.

At the age of sixteen, my entire life changed. My mom was diagnosed with Lymphoma. At this time, it was just she and I living in our home. I had to be my mom's backbone when she didn't have one to hold her head up.

I always knew my goofiness; extra funny and uncontrollable weirdness came from my mom. Before this time, I was kind of embarrassed by it. Once you shave your mom's head at sixteen, your entire life perspective will change! Everything about her now became extra precious and ever so special. Every moment was now to be cherished and filled with gratitude. This was the moment that I decided I wanted to have a better life for my mom and me.

Years after that, I saw her lose two husbands. As she became a widow over and over again and having no estate left for her, I knew it would be up to me. I had to make the life for us, if we were going to have one. Every interview I have ever been on, I got the job. My first was at fifteen and I remember giving my mom, the first check. That action defines my desire to contribute today.

I remember always telling her of our future life and how I always wanted to travel and do things that we never got to do. I always wanted to make good money. As a college student, I worked and played sports.

I desired to be a coach and a teacher and soon realized

that those careers had a ceiling.

Being the money conscious young lady I was, with all the medical attention my parents required, I knew I needed to make more money than they did. I found myself in real estate and fine dining. Giving up my teaching and coaching goals was so hard, but I had to trust my heart.

Once I googled who made the most money in the U.S. it mentioned business owners and investors. I knew then that I needed to own something. Being in real estate, I became aware of who was making the most money very quickly and was eager to learn how to become a broker.

Being told I wouldn't be taught for five years to be a broker by my original real estate broker was probably the best setback that could have happened to me. During that five year wait, I was introduced to a broker at *World Financial Group*. During my first interview, I discovered that they were looking for brokers to build and train agents and teach people how to get in better financial shape.

They helped people save money when they get sick, pass away early, and during a market crash, and I could feel it in my bones that I could use this knowledge! Not to mention to learn how to own my business for life, receive residual income, and get to be a part of something so special. Life with *WFG* has been everything I had been searching for.

And it fits my personality that gets overly excited for the little things. It fits everything in my life, from the captain I once was, to the coach I always wanted to be. It fills my teacher's heart and feeds my entrepreneurship goals. Because of this company, I have peace of mind about not only my mom's retirement but me and everyone I come in contact with! Sometimes I wake up with so much gratitude for the opportunities it has led me to.

Because of WFG, I have had the opportunity to speak at elementary schools, high schools, and even prestigious colleges like USC about financial literacy and what they don't teach us in school about money. I get to teach students of all ages how not avoid the financial burdens that I and most Americans all over the world deal with on a daily basis.

I'm known as an Inspirational Speaker, and I've also been asked to speak for various organizations throughout the U.S. One highlight was the opportunity to speak at the *Council of Igbo States of America on Financial Literacy*.

Having a gift of EXCITEMENT gave me the glue of connection to a subject that can be so hard to talk about. My perspective and life experience as a woman definitely leads the way I make my mark in the financial world.

My grandmother was a huge activist for the *Women's Rights Movement* and walked with Martin Luther King. My stepfather, who is now in heaven, was building businesses in Nigeria for women and assisting orphanages before he passed.

My family's story has led me to the drive I have today. We spearhead women not settling for glass ceilings or being discriminated against, such as being pregnant on the job or being paid less because of sex. This company has the most women in any financial firm, and I truly believe that is something to be so very proud of.

Women have been sworn to the kitchen for so long and are now becoming the household decision makers. We have now been given a chance to have a voice in the financial world like never before.

Here at WFG I get to be the coach I always wanted to be and lead a team that doesn't discriminate and leaves no family behind. My story is not the only one that matters. My adversities have been my lessons. My excitement is my gift. My dreams keep me going. My individuality makes me relatable. My vision is clear, and I look forward to having so much peace of mind and fun along the way!

Top 10 Lessons Learned

1. Money is not the root of evil. The love of money is the root of all evil.

2. You can beat the person who works harder and smarter than you.

3. Love wins.

4. Build each other's strengths and dismiss the weaknesses.

5. This moment only exists now. Be happy in the moment, that's enough. That's all we need.

6. It is not the money that defines your success, it is how you treat people along the way and once you have it that does.

7. Kill them with Kindness.

8. World Class people believe in Servant Leadership

9. People don't follow you just because of where you are but where you are going.

10. Get better, not bitter.

Challenges to Overcome When it comes to challenges in business it reminds me of life. There are always ups and downs because as long as people are involved there will be freedom to make our own decisions. People don't always choose right over wrong or what's best for one might not be best for all.

Becoming better at mastering human connection is one of my ultimate goals. Helping someone with their financial plan and helping people become honest leading entrepreneurs takes a lot of knowledge on how people think and function. I look forward to getting better at all the challenges that come my way with a solution orientated outlook on everything that might feel like a distraction or a down in my career. Understanding human nature will be my forever ongoing class to master!

Keys to my Success

I truly credit my success to my ability to bounce back. Deep down inside, I know that I try every day to do what is best for everyone. Daily I feel like a superhero for the things that we do for families and the opportunity that we get to give to entrepreneurs.

My honest approach to leading my organization is to treat every client and agent in my division just as I treat my mother. I do this because of that view that has been embedded in me since 16: life is too short not to be memorable.

People remember how they feel around you the most, and I intend to leave every human contact with an energy of confidence, love, and kindness. I want to leave them feeling that I am someone that wants to do what is right for all and that I'm on track for something bigger than me.

I also believe my success has a lot to do with my inner joy. I do believe I have a gift of excitement and joy that in the end, money cannot buy. I'm forever grateful for the ability to make someone laugh and feel alive, especially in the pursuit of a better life.

Vision for the Future

Vision for the future is inevitable.

When we create access to resources that can be refilled generation after generation, the possibilities are endless. Before I die, I intend to make sure that every state teaches financial literacy. I will live in a time where we will be so amazed that we went as long as we did without it! I intend to have a company of one hundred thousand licenses, all over the nation. I intend to help spearhead this company to help the U.S. manage the trillions in need.

With the technology of our times and the access to resources where we can be multiple places at once, we intend to be one of the largest financial teams in financial services. I want to be known as the team that looks like the United Nations and represents all walks of life, all ages, and all backgrounds. I plan to put the needs of my team before my own. When my team wins, we all win.

We will be known as "the team who helped bridge the gap between the wealthy and the poor" in this country. We will be the team that moves from the heart and practice what we preach. The ones who did whatever it took to win for our families and financial freedom for all. The ones who didn't give up when the odds were against them.

The ones who still need to define themselves. The ones who have still have more to give and more to learn. Most importantly we will be the team who has generated the most contribution to good in the world. - and will be EXCITED THE ENTIRE TIME DOING IT!

Rose Macias, (909) 567-9667, Sararosereality@gmail.com and ig@global_rosie_rose.com

SHKIRA SINGH

My name is Shkira Singh, and I was born in Walsall, England. My dad was born in India, my mom was born in Africa, and we moved to America in 1982 because we were told this was the land of opportunity.

I was blessed to have watched my dad build a very successful business. He taught me all the ins and outs of his business. My dad poured a lot of time and energy not only into is relationships with his clients, but with his employees as well. He would always make an extra effort to know how they and their families were doing.

I often saw the employees with tears in their eyes and saw how they saw him as more than just a boss, but a mentor who truly had their best interests in mind. My dad led with his heart, and he taught me to lead by that same principle, without worrying about receiving any favors in return.

My father died at the age of fifty-two. I was twenty-four at the time, and at his funeral, dozens of people approached me and told me about the positive impact he had made on their lives. As I listened to the stories told by all these people who loved him, I made an important decision. I knew I wanted to make that same kind of impact on other people. I wanted to do something that truly served a purpose.

I started my career by working in a bank, and thanks to the skills my father taught me, I was able to move up the corporate ladder at a young age. At the same time, I was finishing my undergrad at UCSC and then the International MBA program at San Francisco State University.

I had the incredible opportunity of working as an assistant for one of my mentors, Brad Marshall. He was a top financial advisor. They wanted to know how we were making the big numbers, given that we were such a small branch. Then they asked me to be an advisor for one of the largest branches in the industry.

I became head of the household in July, 2001 and at age twenty-four, I had to generate $6000.00 net a month income to keep the monthly overhead that my parents had. I did not have a chance to even think. I just knew what my dad went through as a business and real estate investor, so I was going to do whatever it keeps my dad's legacy alive as an immigrate from New Delhi.

As it turned out, I had nothing to worry about. I continued advancing up the corporate ladder, keeping my father's work ethic and generous spirit alive. I worked for nineteen years on Wall Street. I owned a wealth management practice that had $150 million in assets and produced over $1,000,000,000 in annual revenue. I sold it for a seven figure price before eventually joining WFG. Today, I continue to do the same quality work I have always done, and I strive to maintain the kinds of compassionate and generous relationships with my clients, as well as my teammates, that my dad would be proud of.

Thank you for the opportunity to share my story. I hope it can be an example of why we at WFG will always continue to serve those who need us most.

Thank you again: *Shkira Singh Global Conscious Leader and founder of Conscious Wealth and TIO.*

Shkira Singh, (626) 244-5887, shkirasingh.consciouswealth@gmail.com

OLIVER AND JAIMIE ZIMAN

OLIVER ZIMAN

I was raised in both Los Angeles and Santa Monica. Life start-ed off rough for me. I came from a single parent home and a hazardous upbringing. Dealing with abandonment from my biological father and growing up in a household of drug ad-dicts created an unstable environment for me. Unfortunately, this adversity was also my "normal". I unconsciously built a tolerance for my surroundings and a survivalist mentality. And I carried a certain degree of numbness with me throughout my upbringing.

Even though I was exposed to a lot of things I should have never seen as a young child, there was another side of my life that was filled with love, and memorable and positive experiences. One of my favorite activities growing up was spending my afternoons and weekends at the *Boys and Girls Club*. Spending time there allowed me to do healthy, fun things, and it gave me an escape from the chaos that was going on at home. I made many friends at the Boys and Girls Club who are still my friends to this day.

After finishing high school, I went to a fashion design school with hopes of starting my own clothing line. Shortly after graduating and working, while also building my clothing line, I soon found out that there was a lot of adversity in the fashion industry to be able to continue this dream. Then, out of the blue and while confronted with this harsh reality, I was prospected and decided to go to a *BPM* to see what *WFG* was about. That was the beginning of a life and career-changing journey.

At the time of being prospected, I was working day and night, sometimes with very little sleep, at two different grocery stores. Although I liked the people I worked with and the customers, I longed to do something more with my life. I made sure to schedule in going to an office to attend BPMs as often as possible, even though sometimes I was exhausted and hadn't had much sleep. Even though I was tired and overworked, there was a persistent draw to WFG, the positive culture of the office, the focus on personal development and helping others, and ease that I found with making money with the company that made me stick around.

I eventually made the decision to quit both of my grocery jobs and go full-time with my business. I knew that if I kept dividing my time between two grocery stores and WFG, I would never really have the success I wanted. I loved working with my clients more than working at the grocery store. So, it was an easy decision.

Oliver Ziman, (310) 413-7945, ziman822@yahoo.com

JAIME ZIMAN

My name is Jaimie Ziman and I was born and raised in Santa Monica. Both of my parents were teachers but divorced when I was two years old. My parents put a huge focus on education and intelligence, and I was a reader from a young age.

My mom raised three children on her own. I remember having a happy childhood, but I also remember spending a lot of time escaping into my own imagination. My mother at times could be distant, so I would spend hours playing alone in my room and truly enjoying it.

Compared to my brother and sister, I was always considered the "good child." Both my brother and sister got into a lot of trouble when I was growing up: stealing, ditching school, drugs, and even gangs. They definitely gave my mom a hard time, but for some reason that I did not understand when I was younger, I always tried my best to be good.

As I got older, I realized that my desire to always be good or "the favorite" was really derived from anxiety. I grew up with a very anxious mother. So in order to please her and to make her happy, I tried to always do what's right. Although that may sound pleasant and easy, it actually stunted my options and kept me in the same occupation for twenty-one years, even though for years I was miserable.

I have been an elementary school educator for twenty-one years and have taught grades Kindergarten to fourth. Although I know that I have done well as a teacher, and that I have positively affected many children's lives, I also knew years ago that I was ready for change.

A few years ago, I considered joining with Oliver in business, but it was always "fear" that held me back. What if I fail? What if I am not perfect? What if the risk is too big? "What if..." played over and over in my mind every time I considered working with Oliver. Even though he would repeatedly tell me that couples who work the business together do far better than working it alone, I resisted.

Finally, this year, Oliver and I made the decision to work together. Even though it's only been a few months, I love it! I love the freedom the business provides, I love talking to people, and I love that I can help families, just like I helped families and children during my twenty-one years of being an educator. In truth, I am still an educator now, but I am educating individuals and families about money.

Lessons Learned and Keys to Success

Some of the major lessons we've learned came from adversity. This business is not easy. If anyone tells you it is, don't believe them! There are ups and downs in our business, but what never wavers is our commitment and focus. We have learned to not listen to nay-sayers, to create vision boards, and to constantly talk about our future. We keep our eyes on our goals and are obsessed with meeting these goals.

What is easy is about this wonderful business is the system that is in place. The system is created to help you succeed. If you follow the system, and find others to follow the system with you, your business will grow substantially. If you fall off the system, your team will as well, and you will not see the success you desire. The great thing about our business is even if you do fall off, you can always easily get back on track. You MUST have drive, focus, and a vision in order to be successful.

It took years for us to develop new habits, a new way of thinking, specific success principles, and a mental shift from employee to business owner. If we could start over knowing what we know now, we would advise the following:

1. Be coachable and do what your mentor suggests that you do (your mentor wants the best for you!).

2. Just do it! Act at the speed of instruction; don't spend a lot of time thinking too much (it will slow your own progress and you'll get caught up in the "what ifs" that we mentioned before).

3. Be consistent with mastering the fundamentals. The system was written by the founders of our company for one simple reason: it works! The founders share exactly what you need to do to build a strong and enduring business. We have seen so many people struggle (including ourselves) because there was a focus away from the proven system.

4. Be committed. The commitment to doing the work is a critical component. What's the work? Making many telephone calls every day, personally recruiting every

month, building a team, driving licensing, creating a "do it first" mentality in your associates, and helping families with our products every day, week, month, and year. This will increase the results of both you AND your team.

5. Create a culture and environment that people enjoy being a part of. Be kind, have fun, and enjoy the journey together.

6. And last, the biggest success principle we can share with you is this: have a specific written plan about what you want. Set goal deadlines for yourself, know exactly how you're going to get to those goals and accomplish them, and share those goals with your mentor to keep yourself accountable. Read your goals multiple times a day out loud with passion and conviction and be obsessed with these goals until the job gets done.

Our future looks incredibly bright. Our vision is to build a massive distribution of licensed agents across North America and Canada. We are focused on helping as many people as possible to also achieve financial independence for their *own* families.

We both come from humble beginnings and have always envisioned living a fulfilled life of love, happiness, and internal peace. We are building great memories together with our family and our friends. We are grateful for ALL that God has and will continue to do for us. We wish you the best success in this business.

Jaimie Ziman, (310) 892-0795,
jzimanvirtuitymanagement@gmail.com

Jen Madamba-Bailey

I joined the company in 2011. I have a background in Human Resources and Administration in non-profits as well as schools for about nine years. Coming from an Asian background, it was instilled in me from a young age that the only way to success was through going to school, getting a few degrees, and obtaining a great job with benefits.

As the youngest out of five older brothers, I was ambitious and wanted so much out of life: lots of money, control of my time and income, a beautiful family, and to see the world on my own terms.

I have always been a great student, graduating Summa Cum Laude at my CSUN graduation. School was fortunately easy for me, but after completing my undergraduate degree, I was lacking direction. I changed my major a few times, and I thought more schooling would lead me to better opportunities. I then decided I would go to graduate school. I was accepted to UCLA and completed my graduate coursework with the intention of going to Law School.

After interning at a law firm in Los Angeles, I quickly realized I was not cut out to be an attorney. I craved rolling my sleeves up and sitting kneecap to kneecap with individuals and families and contributing to their physical and emotional growth.

I ended up at YMCA first as a dance instructor, then dabbled into tumbling with the younger students, fitness instructor, then later as a Community Resource Director. At this point, I fell in love with the community and service.

After a few years of such rewarding work of watching kids & adults grow in such a positive environment, the cost of living finally caught up with me. I knew I wanted more in life. I saw the families I served had large beautiful homes, fancy cars, and what appeared to be a stress-free lifestyle.

Then I soon realized that the lifestyle I imagined was not going to be sustained by my non-profit salary. I was in search of something bigger and better but was not sure what that looked like career wise.

In 2008, I met my spouse, David Bailey. I would never imagine that eleven years later, we would not only be best friends and spouses, but business and life partners building both an amazing family and business.

During the time we met, I learned that David was also dissatisfied. He was laid off from teaching several times, and he too was in search of a better life and career. A better life where we had more control of our time and income. We knew we wanted a lifestyle that would allow us to travel, build our dream home, not worry about money, but also give us the opportunity to help both our families financially. As a result, he was dabbling in real estate in efforts of a career change. I joined him in the real estate venture shortly after.

In the midst of getting into real estate, we faced a few challenges. One being that it is a competitive field and the inventory is limited. As we were getting started, David was introduced to the company by way of the financial education that was offered.

David and I were first clients with our firm, and we needed a financial plan. When I was taught key financial concepts, I saw the value and great need for financial literacy. Disturbed and excited, I gained an understanding that implementing simple financial concepts, I could improve my financial situation.

After becoming clients, David was asked to come to a company event. He decided to come on-board. He asked me to come to the office in support of him. I came in kicking and screaming because I was focused on our real estate venture, and we had spent thirty thousand dollars on training materials and mentoring.

I didn't want anything else on my plate. I found out that David was introduced to the company ten years prior but was not ready for the opportunity. I was intrigued. After careful consideration and empowered with changing my financial trajectory, I decided to join David in business.

In retrospect, I look back and have found three prominent lessons from the business and through my own personal development:

1. I'm not done working on myself. I have learned that each level of success I achieve and each phase in life demands a better version of myself. This process is continuous and painful, but I have never looked back and regretted increasing my capacity. I have always been grateful that I overcame and struggled forward. Even when I had doubts, I pushed through and persevered because I knew it would get me closer to my dreams and goals.

2. Life wasn't meant for me to be mediocre and just settle to pay bills and grind for the rest of my life. My family deserves better. With our opportunity, I dare to dream big and design the life God meant for me to be able to contribute and impact not only my family, but countless others along the way.

3. I CAN have it all- an incredible marriage, a closer relationship with God, a strong family held by values, integrity, crazy amounts of love & fun, and an amazing business that supports all of this.

Some struggles I have gone through:

1. In the beginning, I didn't think I was cut out to be a financial professional, so I sought mentorship and listened to people who had a great marriage, who were successful in the business and I gave myself a shot.

My thought process was if what they are telling me is true, then I will be better for it - financially, spiritually, and emotionally. Through much doubt, I stumbled forward, learned from mistakes and the mistakes of others and the lessons learned held heavier weight than my temporary discomfort and momentary disappointment. I decided to move forward.

2. In the later stages in my career, I also suffered from mommy guilt. As we started our family, I knew we were not where we wanted to be and much work still needed to be done. I often wondered if I came back to work too soon, but I looked at the positive side. My baby was with me at my office. I had the luxury of setting up a playpen and a ball pit for him to be entertained. As I saw clients, he slept next to me. As I made calls, I nursed him and shut the door and pumped.

As we met with the team, I had a trusted village there (in addition to my awesome parents and aunts). As I sat with guests, I knew he was in wonderful hands. As we had our second baby, same thing. However, when I'm in the office I get work done. When the baby needs my attention, he has it. I am growing my capacity as a mother and a business owner. I am constantly growing. This opportunity has allowed me to take the time I need with my kids- in and out of the office. I still allocate a family day within the week. David and I have weekly scheduled date nights. We are a work in progress, but I am grateful for this business supports a strong family core and my important relationship with my husband.

Our vision for the future is expanding our business throughout the country. We have offices in all fifty states so we can be a blessing to others. We were blessed with two boys. We are sending my sons to the best schools and being the best role models for them is all that really matters. We are building and leaving a legacy for our family. David will conquer all mountains around the world snowboarding & I will be sipping a beverage in the *Maldives* while I wait for the boys to return from the snow.

Jen Bailey, (818) 288-7317,
jen.madamba@yahoo.com

DAVID BAILEY

I was born and raised in Los Angeles, California. I have four sisters, three younger and one older. My dad was a computer engineer and my mother worked as a teacher. At an early age, my dad worked long hours and my mother worked as a teacher. She also took care of the household.

At age 15, I took my first summer job. I worked 8 hours a day, making $3.65 an hour. I took home $200 every two weeks. It was exciting, because I could now buy all the things I wanted but could never afford before. I did not have to ask my parents for money. I also did odd jobs in the neighborhood such as cutting the grass and working for my friend's parents in the

catering business. I understood that if I wanted or needed anything, I had to work for it.

I got my first credit card from Circuit City. Now I would
be able to buy my mother a stereo for Christmas. The card was
mailed to the house, and when my dad found out I now had a
credit card, he warned me, "David, you have credit now. Don't
abuse it."

My parents taught me many things, but they were unable
to teach me about how money worked. But I *did* know how
to work hard. I had many jobs. I worked for the Los Angeles
Dodgers, I did public relations work for Earth, Wind and Fire;
I worked at Olive Garden while I was a full-time student. Simply put, I was exhausted all the time. Eventually, I graduated
from California State University, Northridge with a degree in
communications. I started working part-time for LAUSD as a
substitute teacher. From there, I was offered a permanent position and have been working for LAUSD ever since.

I was earning about $60k/year. I bought the things I want-
ed to buy, and I did the things I wanted to do. However, my
spending habits caught up with me. I struggled for many years
when it came to finances. The hardship was real! Imagine paying for a trip and still not able to go because all of your debt
has caught up with you. That happened to me. Not only that, I
was not able to afford a place to stay. I had to stay at my sister's
house and sleep on her couch.

After a while, I somehow was able to move out of my sister's house. A friend of mine owned property and needed a rent-
er, so he let me rent the place. I still struggled. I was late on the
rent several times because I was laid off of work three times. I
figured things could not get any worse. Unfortunately, it did.

My mother had been sick for many years. My dad had difficulties paying her medical bills and asked for assistance. He was told that he would be unable to get help because he had a job, he owned a home, and he had a retirement fund. My dad depleted his retirement, lost his job, and lost the house I was raised in. My mother watched all the things she worked hard for being taken away. She passed away in 2008 at the age of 60.

I hit rock bottom. I had no idea where my life was going, or if it would even go anywhere. Still, when I found work, I made decent money, but I had too much debt and did not know what to do. I was tired of having money issues and wanted to solve them for good. I started asking everyone I knew if they knew anyone who could help me with finances. Finally, a young man named Blake Shepard gave me a call.

He told me that he worked for a company called WFG and that my oldest sister referred him to me. He worked in the financial industry and would like to share some information with me about how money worked. This was information I desperately needed, so I agreed to meet with him.

When we met, he and Oliver Ziman gave me all the financial information I was hungry for. They took some notes about my financial situation and came back a few days later with some recommendations.

I was impressed with their knowledge and relieved that I was going to learn how to manage my money. I wished that someone would have told me sooner about these easy techniques, but maybe I needed to wait until now to learn it. Maybe there was a reason why it took so long to happen. Anyhow, I can honestly say that these gentlemen from WFG truly helped me out when I needed them most. In 2011, I joined the com-

pany and planted my flag, and I have to say, I've never regretted that decision. My crusade is to empower others with the
information on how money works.

Keys to Personal Success

First: Finding something you're passionate about is a
must. Even though you must make money to stay in business,
it does not mean anything if you are not able to bless others. I
find that in this business, I am able to bless others but also be
compensated very well for what I do.

Second: Stretch your vision. Read books that will help
with personal development. It will stretch your vision. It is an
absolute must.

Third: Putting God in my life has helped me and my family grow spiritually. No matter what your faith is, you must allow yourself to grow spiritually.

Fourth: Have a mentor. My mentors have guided me,
held me accountable for mistakes and successes, and have
helped me remain focused on the task at hand. It's one of the
best things you can do for yourself. All successful people have
mentors.

Lastly, stay the course. Do not get discouraged. So many
times people have told me that they've tried to do what I did
and it didn't work for them. And I've always told them that the
only reason it *didn't* work for them is because they quit. The
solution is to never quit.

Challenges to Overcome

One of the major challenges to overcome is other people. Other people can be very negative and will try to talk you out of your dreams, only because they lack the drive to pursue their own. Don't allow other people to steal your dreams.

Also, rejection happens, and it's draining. You must develop a thick skin. No one wants to be rejected. However, experiencing it will make you a stronger person in the long run.

Vision for My Future

My wife and I see our business expanding throughout the country. We envision offices in all 50 states so that we can educate and empower people all over. We can be a blessing to others. We were blessed with two boys. Sending my sons to the best schools and being the best role models for them is all that really matters. Leaving a legacy for my family is my most important goal.

David Bailey, (310) 863-2862,
Bailey0707@gmail.com

BEN KLINGER

When dad was in the hospital, at one point he was moved to a room with a window facing northwest. It was a much brighter room than his previous room had been. Those first few days in the hospital were rough. Mom, Tali and I were struggling to come to terms with the gravity of Dad's deteriorating health.

So when I walked in to visit Dad in this new room, imagine my delight to see him awake, alert and talkative. More so than I'd seen him in months! He was filled with excitement and optimism, which was infectious (as his energy always was).

He proceeded to describe a meeting he just had, and an exciting business opportunity that was offered to him. As he turned towards the window, and then back to me, he pointed to the building outside the window, yet struggled to find the words to accurately convey what he was trying to communicate. One thing was clear, though: it had something to do with that building outside the window.

I was perplexed. What was he trying to say? Could he have met with someone here at the hospital? Maybe. Who knew? Dad never stopped thinking about ways to build a successful business. Always the entrepreneur, he spent his time looking for solutions to societal problems. His ideas were fantastic, and for the last several years, each one centered around real estate, which was his wheelhouse.

In retrospect, I now realize a big part of his motivation for these business ideas was his own financial struggle. He was operating in perpetual survival mode, and had no money, time or energy to see his idea through and launch it into a business. He was too concerned with having enough money to pay his bills each month.

Standing in that hospital room, I quickly realized this "meeting" he had about an opportunity may have been a dream. A figment of his incredibly creative imagination. Still, I was intrigued and I asked him all sorts of questions to try and figure out exactly what he was talking about. More importantly, I was hopeful that he had turned a corner with his health and was starting to recover.

Sadly, this surge of energy was not part of a recovery. Dad passed away about two weeks later. As you can imagine, this was a very difficult time for me. Little did I know this experience - watching my dad's financial struggles and the ensuing decline of his health - would set the stage for my new career path with WFG that began about a year and a half later.

Because of what my dad and our family had gone through, I was open enough to look into an opportunity in "financial services" when I got a call from Ryan Ademy. I knew I needed to educate myself about how money really works, as well as the importance of planning ahead.

I was given the opportunity to join the company part-time mainly for that reason. As I learned more, I saw the tremendous need for everybody to learn these things. I thought about my family, my friends, my network. How many of them had a specific plan for their future? How many knew what compound interest was? Even if they did know, were they implementing it in their lives? I knew most weren't. What if I could be the one to share this valuable information with them? What if I was the one who could make a real difference in their lives?

About three years into my WFG career, I was given an opportunity to rent the corner office in Virtuity's Tarzana location for my team. That particular branch had grown to about 20 active associates. I jumped at the chance.

I was introduced to a young man named Ryan Ademy, thanks to our family friend Janet. Ryan gave me an overview of this business, and I came on board. Little did I know, Ryan would soon become my first mentor.

Leadership is one of the greatest gifts of all. It can be cultivated, yes. I believe some people can also be born with it. Ryan has it, and WFG helped him cultivate it. It was Ryan who asked me one of the most pivotal questions of my life. He asked me to describe my wildest dream, the dream that seems almost out of reach, yet would feel amazing to achieve. I thought for a moment, and I thought of my family.

I told Ryan I would love to fly my mom and sister to Italy for their dream vacation. They had always wanted to go there, so Ryan challenged me. He said if I really wanted to make it happen, I had to give myself a timeline. I said within 2 years. Then he challenged me one more time. He said accountability is key and encouraged me to call my sister and tell her that I'll take her and mom to Italy within 2 years. So I called her my sister and told her exactly that.

Time went on, and I had a lot of growing to do. In retrospect, I now know that this business is really a personal development program with a powerful compensation package attached. To become successful in WFG, you have to believe in yourself as a leader to some extent. Even when there are still "layers of the onion" to peel back, old identities and limiting beliefs to strip away, you can still see yourself as a magnificent, successful human being. You define your identity by the future vision of yourself, rather than confine yourself to the person you were in the past.

I drifted for a few years, lost touch with my goals and who I was not only as a person, but as a brother and a son. After a couple not-so-successful years, I started losing enthusiasm for my Italy dream. I started to let it go and accept that I probably wasn't going to be able to make it happen like I had hoped.

But I bounced back, after working as a party DJ for a Caribbean cruise liner. DJ work was something I did every so often. This particular cruise lasted for a month, and I had all kinds of exciting experiences that I experienced alone. And as fun as those experiences were, I realized that none of the people I truly loved had been able to come with me on this amazing trip. And that's what it was really about: sharing beautiful moments with the people you love.

I returned home to LA in late May 2017 with a renewed sense of vigor. I knew this incredible business was waiting for me to grab it by the horns and run with it! Shortly after my return I spoke with Ryan, excited about my decision and the future.

But as it turned out, Ryan and his wife Jessica had decided to move back to Florida, where Ryan grew up. I was devastated. My business coach would not be here to help me take my business to the next level.

I had two options. Take ownership of this thing or quit. I had already made my decision, so I supported Ryan doing what he had to do, and he supported me doing what I had to do. We ended up proving that the WFG system works, even in bizarre ways. We set up weekly coaching calls, and he mentored me from 3,000 miles away. I have to say, he did an incredible job. Six months later, I made $25k in only 2 months, I got promoted to MD, and I was asked to speak for almost 2 hours at the office of a multi-millionaire, seven-figure earner, WFG legend John Shin. Hey, if a party DJ can do it, so can you!

Now that I knew what I was doing, I knew it was my duty to share this business platform with people. I started telling my girlfriend, my associates, the whole office; I told my niece, nephew, and Uncle Benny: "I am *going* to take you all to Italy." I wrote it in my business plan and life vision and reread it almost every day. I even made an Italy Trip 2019 Dream Board!

In April 2019, I bought 8 round-trip tickets from LAX to Rome. After buying the tickets, I thought of my half-sister,

Cassia who lives part-time in Florence, and part-time in Israel for work. I'd never met her, but I remembered my dad used to speak to her on the phone periodically when I was growing up. I emailed her, and it turned out that she would be returning from Israel three days before our trip ended. Could there be an even bigger purpose to this trip than I first realized?

We traveled all over central Italy and Tuscany, stopping in ancient rural villages and historical cities like Siena, Florence, Lucca and Pisa. Joyce and I went to the amazing Cinque Terre for a few days while my mom and sister's family went to Venice. Our trip would end with three days in Rome. Our sister Cassia and her partner Massimo cleared their schedule to join us for every meal during those last two days in Rome. A truly remarkable family reunion. We love them. My niece and nephew got to meet them, too! Thanks to this trip, our family grew. It's hard to put the value of that into words.

In retrospect, the sequence of events makes so much sense. I can clearly see all the things that needed to happen in order for me to be where I am today. But when you're living your day-to-day life, you're just riding the wave. I don't remember all the work, all the driving, phone calls, appointments, trainings, no-show appointments, etc. Instead, I remember the victories. I *choose* to remember the victories, and I'm grateful for the whole process. I'm grateful for my team, who put their faith in me as a leader and worked their butts off to make sure we hit every deadline while I was on vacation. That's an entirely different story that deserves its own chapter one day.

In what other company can you take your family on their dream vacation, get paid thousands of dollars while you're there, and come home to a massive promotion?! Thank you,

Team Willpower! I am truly filled with gratitude.

To my incredible team, whether you're brand new or you've been with me from the beginning, I want you to know that you absolutely can create the life you desire. It is never too late, or too early, to redefine your identity and step boldly into a new adventure. This is your time.

Ben Klinger, (323)420-8945, Benklingerwfg@gmail.com Instagram: @Ben.n.klinger

SHARON GRIFFIN

We often hear how important it is to leverage leadership in business. Well, I also think we should leverage our life work and experiences to help us build successful businesses. As leaders, we should seek to understand how people think and behave. People are the most valuable asset any organization has, and they can make or break a business.

My time spent learning the ins and outs of corporate America

I spent thirty plus years as a risk management profession-al. My experience in corporate America gave me the professional foundation that I needed to become a successful business owner and now broker with *Virtuity Financial Partners/ World Financial Group.*

I'm very proud of my past accomplishments as a corporate executive and a business owner. I am also proud to be the current president of a nonprofit organization that focuses on teaching the underserved and underemployed segments marketable skills that can position them for success. I believe that changing an individual's financial wellbeing could have a direct impact on improving the financial wellbeing and economics of their respective communities. I am passionate in promoting financial literacy, education, and entrepreneurship.

Too many people fail because they're afraid to take risks or are too concerned about what other people might say or think about them. The richest man in the world has stated, "If you can't tolerate critics, don't do anything new or interesting" – Jeff Bezos.

Small businesses are the key to building strong communities and each of us can play a vital role in helping people succeed if we, as leaders, have the right mindset.

Now a little bit about my journey.

I came from the beautiful southern California city of San Diego. As a matter of fact, the majority of my extended family are still there. My expansion goals are that one day, God willing, I may even return there.

When I was in grade school, my Dad moved my siblings and me to the suburbs of Los Angeles county, and after high school, I moved to Orange County to attend college. Shortly after graduating from *CSUF*, I pursued and landed a sales job with a small and little known (just kidding) insurance company named *Transamerica*. I lasted just long enough to get licensed and receive my first month's paycheck. I quickly recognized that going door to door selling AD&D insurance was not for me.

So imagine what I must have thought when I arrived at my very first BPM and saw the *Transamerica* sign on the wall!

Talk about going full circle. As I was on my way out the door, the person that invited me stopped me so he could introduce me to my soon-to-be SMD who "just wanted to say goodbye and thank me for coming." I never would have expected to be where I am today given that history!

But going back to my history, after leaving *Transamerica* as an insurance agent in my early days, still interested in the world of finance, I went to work for an insurance broker. After a year or so, I transitioned to another type of financial institution by accepting a job at *Bank of America*. From that point on, I worked with various types of financial institutions and later with an accounting firm where I became a risk management professional and business consultant for some of the largest and most well-known financial institutions and nonprofit organizations in the country. As I became more knowledgeable and skilled, my passion grew. I loved it!

I learned how different businesses ran, how they increased their profitability and how they streamlined operations. I also learned that "employees" were often casualties of the decisions that were made to accomplish a lot of the strategic goals the companies had.

During those years, I became more determined to use my education, expertise and experience to make a difference in people's lives, to give them options in case they were ever on the wrong end of their employer's decisions. After having become a recipient of one of those decisions myself, I utilized my corporate training and launched a bookkeeping and tax preparation business. My business eventually expanded to include consulting services, which I branded as *SDG Consulting*.

These were uncharted waters and as a single parent, it wasn't easy in the beginning. There were times when I doubted myself, but I was surrounded by the support of friends and mentors who encouraged me to continue. It was hard work and quite risky, but it was sooo worth it.

When I look back on those days, I understand now what it took to win and what that looks like. You have to work to win. "Don't be afraid. Be focused. Be determined. Be hopeful. Be empowered" says Michelle Obama. I would encourage us all to follow the proven wisdom that history has engraved in granite. A career coach has also stated "Success is not a wheel that needs to be reinvented. But It does need to be "tried" to be proven." – Brynda Woods

Over the years, I have mentored and taught the underserved and underemployed marketable skills. I have helped many on their paths to become entrepreneurs. Showing them how to create additional streams of income in order to eradicate debt which supports a more meaningful lifestyle for both themselves and their families.

It's interesting (even to me), how what I have been doing for the last twenty-plus years, I'm doing here with *WFG* with just a slightly different platform. Today, I can say, I am one of the most fortunate beings in the world as I have both identified and am fulfilling my purpose in life. I'm passionate about helping others and think I've found the perfect vehicle through which to accomplish it.

Lessons Learned

I've learned that sometimes, in order to alter your perspective, you have to alter your environment. Earlier this year, I was feeling stuck and underwhelmed, so I took a trip to London to clear my head. This was a drastic change in my emotional as well as my physical environment. It was there that I was encouraged, strengthened and recognized that it was time to make changes. It was in that foreign (uncommon) environment that I recognized that the bigger the chasm (profound difference between a thing or people), the bigger the bridge you have to build.

Once settled, it was that thought, that idea, that motivated me to relocate and open my own office in South Pasadena. What an absolute delightful, invigorating and rewarding decision that has become, no less disguised as a challenge! As research has verified, this move has opened up a new market for myself and my teammates.

We're out hustling every day because we want to introduce our products and services to this community. When you're doing what you love and seeing your goals and dreams come alive and falling into place, you can't help but be excited.

Another thing I've learned is not to take things personally or take myself too seriously. I know I can't control everything that happens but can only operate with strategy and integrity. What I can control is how I respond to situations outside of my control. I try to be positive, take (and give) constructive criticism and learn from my mistakes, as well as those of others.

I also know success cannot be gained without ups and downs, starts and stops, and wins and losses. The key here is to be flexible and adaptable, never get too low or too high, and most of all, never quit on your goals and dreams. Seek stability at each level you achieve while planning on the next. Know what you want, why you want it, and then be wise enough to network and brainstorm with others who have successfully done it before and learn how to go about achieving it.

I've learned not to be afraid to change but to embrace change as a necessary tool for destroying "sameness". Modern day processes and technologies make it necessary to change. Although I'm proud of my past accomplishments, I fully understand that in order to progress, I must learn new ways of doing business and adapt to the many different platforms and systems available and accessible to us. The best advice to be offered includes that you must be constantly learning new things and how to use new tools. Ever evolving.

Keys to success

I know without a doubt, having an accountability partner has contributed to my success in my businesses. Setting goals and reporting progress daily has increased my activity and productivity but not diminish my enthusiasm.

Making my intentions known is another key to my success. Having goals is one thing but keeping them to yourself is playing small. You have to be transparent and not afraid of having someone hold you accountable for the commitments you make. It takes courage to succeed.

I've learned to be reflective and look for ways to continuously improve myself. I read and listen to books and podcasts on leadership regularly. I believe in setting goals, measuring my progress, having a strong work ethic, and being disciplined.

One of the books I'm reading is W. Clement Stone's *"Believe and Achieve - 17 Principles of Success"*. Amongst the principles, he discusses having a positive attitude, learning from defeat, teamwork, applied faith and self-discipline. These principles resonate with me because I believe these principles must be active in you and reflected in your business if you intend to excel or grow.

"If you don't know where you're going, any road will get you there" says Cheshire Cat. I remember when I decided to pursue my first promotion, I sat with my supervisor and went over the promotion guidelines. Then one by one, accomplished them all. I did that my whole career and know it works. When I'm pursuing something, I try to stay positive because it helps me stay focused as negativity tends to create mind fog. I surround myself with like-minded people and keep the naysayers away. I also measure my progress and keep my eye on the timeline as well as the milestones.

I also know the value of teamwork. In business, you have to communicate and keep the team informed. Having a team focused on common goals is an incredible thing to accomplish but it is also challenging to a leader. The thing I learned is that you can only get so far by yourself and at some point, as a leader, you have to build others and also help them achieve their goals. Ronald Reagan said "The greatest leader is not necessarily the one who does the greatest things. He is the one that gets people to do the greatest things." My goal is to become that great leader who builds great leaders.

It's imperative to invest in yourself. Whether you attend seminars, webinars, and industry events, you must place value in personal development. No matter how great you think you are, you can be better. And the better you are, the more people will want to follow you, which is the only true evidence of leadership. You must add value to be valued.

Vision for the Future:

My goal is to support and promote three frontline senior marketing directors by 2021. My vision for SDG Consulting and WFG is to become known as a premier financial services company offering a complete array of financial products and services to individuals and small businesses.

My nonprofit organization will continue delivering financial literacy, education and training. My goal is to open six training centers (three in southern California, one each in Texas, North Carolina, and Florida). The centers will be headed by dedicated financial professionals who are committed to improving the financial wellbeing of the communities they serve. The training centers will host workshops, seminars, classes and vocational training for future entrepreneurs and leaders. In this, I know we will make this world a better place.

Principal, SDG Consulting
Senior Marketing Director, World Financial Group

Sharon Griffin, (626) 394-7205, Sharon.griffin@sdgconsults.com

LESTER BARON

I grew up on the tiny island of Dominica, located in the Eastern Caribbean. I left at the age of 15, leaving both my mom and dad behind to pursue a better life in California. I moved to L.A. and began attending West Los Angeles College. While there, I met a woman named Lina Brown who became a close friend. She encouraged me to apply to UCLA, one of the most prestigious schools in the world.

So I applied. And after finishing community college at the

young age of seventeen, I was accepted into UCLA. During my third year in university, my father passed away suddenly, and I flew back to the Caribbean to spend time with my family. Within seven months after my father's passing, my family lost everything.

It took my parents over forty years to build their assets and losing everything was a complete shock. My family was devastated, and when I returned to the U.S. after a year at home, I decided I never wanted to see that again. I never wanted to see my family lose everything they owned, ever again. I never wanted them to experience that kind of loss ever again. After returning to UCLA, I received my bachelor's in psychology. With a degree under my belt, I decided I was going to pursue a full-time career, so I started working for the city of Los Angeles. I worked in animal services, general services. That eventually led to a "career" at the DWP (Department of Water and Power).

Life seemed to be great. I received overtime, a pension, contributed to a 401k, etc. They were paying for my master's degree in civil engineering, but I wasn't fulfilled. I found myself yearning for a career where I could truly help people. One of my coworkers referred me to his uncle, who worked at World Financial Group, and I decided to check it out.

I was hired, and I began working for WFG in September 2008. I met a man named Rudy, who became my friend and mentor in the business. From the moment we met, he always recognized my potential in this business and nurtured my growth, patiently teaching me as I progressed through the firm. I will always be grateful to Rudy for taking me under his wing when I was green and new to the business. His passion for helping people has always been inspiring and has even rubbed off on me.

When I began working at the company, I was only working part-time. Early in my career, Rudy took me out to a company event in Palm Springs. Rudy promised me this event was going to help me understand our business not just from a practical and financial perspective, but from an emotional perspective as well. And he was right! I learned so much from the speakers and presenters, I was so moved by their stories and their passion for helping people change their lives for better and forever that I decided to quit my master's program, and instead focus one-hundred percent of my time and energy on this business.

From that moment forward, I became a full-fledged entrepreneur. As I devoted more and more time to the company, I got a little taste of what it felt like to be a mentor to others. I was also mentored by others as well. Hanna Horenstein, for example, served as one of my mentors, and I have to say, she is one world-class mentor. She was a great mentor, not just because of her enormous business success, but because of her incredible example as a mother, a wife, and a businesswoman. Based on everything she has accomplished at our firm, Virtuity, I would go on record as saying she is in the upper echelons of female entrepreneurs. I cannot thank her enough for all the instruction and support she has given me.

Once I started devoting my time and energy to being a full-time entrepreneur, I started earning a six-figure salary and was starting to build an agency. I married my beautiful wife, and we opened an office together in Sherman Oaks, California. We moved out to Rancho Cucamonga, (where we currently reside) and we branched out, making partners in Torrance,

South Pasadena, Washington state, Dallas, Arizona, Idaho, Minnesota, Florida, Georgia, Tennessee, etc. Virtuity gave us the freedom of being in control of our time, which is the most precious resource of all.

As our firm became successful, my wife and I decided we wanted to commit our lives to serving others. That's what we've done since the beginning, and neither of us have looked back or regretted our decision for a moment.

The best advice I can give to someone who wants to follow in our footsteps is:

1. build a big agency as fast as you can. Bring as many people onboard during the early stages as you can.
2. track what's happening with those partners. You are running a real business, and as you progress, it's important to know where your colleagues and partners are in their own success stories. Are you guiding them as best as you could? Are you helping them learn the fundamentals of your trade? You need to realize that from the first day someone jumps onboard with you and your business, you are a leader and must behave accordingly.
3. build your leadership skills. If you're going to be managing and instructing a team, then you'd better have some excellent leadership skills. If you look at yourself and you think *I don't have what it takes to become a leader*, then you'd better get what it takes as soon as possible.

To anyone who is already a seasoned veteran of our business, I would simply advise to keep improving yourself. Keep changing. Don't become stagnant; don't become complacent.

It is vital to your success in your chosen field to continue changing and growing. You must have a strong desire to become a better version of yourself.

Remember, this journey to success is not only about you. It is also about everyone you help, everyone you impact, and how you can change the world for the better. All the clients who walk through your doors looking for help - they are your legacy.

Thanks to Virtuity, I have a new life. I have freedom. Control. I get to create my own schedule, and I get to help people improve their lives. Thank you to Hanna and thank you everyone else who has helped me throughout my journey. I know they can do the same for you.

Lester Baron, (310) 617-4438,
lebbaron@yahoo.com

KIRSTEN BARON

I'm a first generation American. My parents immigrated to the United States from a tiny Island in the Caribbean called Dominica. I was born and raised in Southern California, Rancho Cucamonga.

Growing up, I always visualized and had visions of the kind of life that I wanted in the future. It was important for me to do something, where I felt like I was helping people. I wanted to have the feeling of fulfillment, as I went through school and I readied for college as well as while I was in college. I was exploring different avenues, trying to figure out what I wanted to do.

Again, something that I knew that I loved doing was helping people and working with kids. Throughout my entire life I have worked with children in my church ministry. I've always been involved in this work. And so, it was in college that I came across the field of social work. What I liked about social work, was that I was doing just that... helping people. I went into that field.

I got my degree in social work, and I ended up working for the Department of Children and Family Services. It was not something that I wanted to do. I considered the nonprofit route to allow me to be more of myself. But regardless of what I wanted or where I saw myself, the first job that I got was, again, working for Los Angeles County Department of Children and Family Services.

I was assigned to what is called *"The Emergency Response Unit."* It was literally my job to go into people's homes anytime there was a report made for possible child abuse or neglect. I had to investigate the allegations and then remove the child from the home if it came to that.

I quickly realized that this was not the long-term, or even short-term, path for me. Even though at the time I was grateful: I had a "secure job," and it was in my field, which is very rare nowadays.

But again, I knew that it was not something that I could see myself doing forever. At the time, I had actually begun dating the person who is now my husband. It was him who introduced me to what he was doing, World Financial Group.

What stuck out to me the first time, when I came to one of the corporate overviews, was to learn more about the company and the opportunity to earn additional income. But also, I learned the education aspect.

I was fortunate enough to come from a household where, at a very young age, my parents, and specifically my mom, always taught me to save money and be financially responsible. She taught me not to splurge and spend money on unnecessary things. As a result, I grew up with pretty good savings habits.

I bought my first car when I was nineteen years old. I paid cash that I had saved specifically for my first car. I had those habits. So when I was first introduced to the education side of World Financial Group, it was something that made sense to me.

I sat down with someone who gave me my own personal financial analysis and financial review. I was able to implement those things to protect myself and protect my family while also saving money with long-term tax benefits.

Now, even though the opportunity was appealing to me, and I saw it as a great opportunity to earn additional income, I didn't necessarily yet have the belief or the insight that it was something that I could do. Coming from a social work background, I thought that social work was a field I would stay in - even though I didn't like my job. I always had plans to eventually go back to school. I planned to get my master's degree in social work. This would then broaden my horizons and broaden the opportunities of what I could do in that field.

Even with my intention to stay in social work, I ended up working part-time with Lester in the company. I mostly helped him and supported him, but my life really turned around. And what really opened my eyes to the opportunities within this company was when I attended my first company event called *Wealth Bowl* in January of 2012. At that event, I saw people from all kinds of backgrounds, and I saw people that came from similar situations as myself.

I saw people that were older; people that were younger; and a wide variety of those people were winning. What that event did for me was really open my eyes to what this company is about. It helped me to see the bigger picture.

I knew that we were helping people. I knew that it was a good opportunity to make money, but what I found were the core values. They really stuck out to me because I came from a work environment in my position with the County, where there were no core values. This is kind of surprising. You would think there would be in that kind of job. But I came from a very negative work environment. There was not a lot of support and a lot of backstabbing. It was just a very toxic environment.

Coming into *Virtuity Financial Partners* and *World Financial Group*, I could see the positive environment. I could see how the focus was on encouraging people and doing the right thing. I could also see that the building of character and having integrity were values that were important to me and also important to Virtuity and WFG. And yet I didn't see it in my own workplace in the County.

Wealth Bowl also helped me identify something within myself that was lingering in the back of my head. But coming into a platform where I saw other people actually bringing the best out of each other inspired me to want to do the same.

I saw people winning and then I realized that I wanted to

win, too. I wanted to be on stage. I wanted to be able to not just help people but influence people and be a voice for people who looked like me; who didn't look like me; who had the insecurities that I had growing up; all the while showing others that it is possible to fulfill your true potential. They showed me it is possible to bring the best out of yourself and to be a leader that inspires rather than commands.

That's what I saw at my first *Wealth Bowl*. And that's when I really made the decision to fully support my husband and to jump on board with this company, both logically and emotionally. I started working part-time. It was still tough balancing both things. But in February of 2015, I left my full-time job with the County. The time had come to jump full-time into *World Financial Group* and *Virtuity*.

That following month, my husband and I had more cash flow than we had ever had before. We were making more already than what I was making annually at my job. Our cash flow in one month was a direct reflection of the people that we were helping. This made a huge impact on me but also led to other realizations in my journey.

Throughout my journey in the company, there were other pivotal moments that helped me identify my "why" in the business and make clear why I knew this was the right place for me. I found a place where I felt at home and encouraged. Where I felt like I could utilize my strengths AND it was something that I wanted to do. I felt like I was becoming the leader that I saw myself as while simultaneously getting the opportunity to create the life I dreamt of.

There were things that I saw in my own personal life that I knew that I would be able to address in this company. For example, there was one point, and this was a few years later, when I was driving home to my parents' house. At the time, my husband and I were living with them temporarily for a few months. We were full-time in the business, and it was going great. I drove home one night, and it was very late.

Now my dad has been self-employed for many, many years and has a vending machine route that he runs. I grew up seeing my dad having to work all the time, because there's a difference between being self-employed and being a business owner. That was something else that being a part of World Financial Group taught me. What I saw in my household was my dad having to work all the time, six, seven days a week. He was too stressed to take time away, to go on vacation because he was concerned about who was going to take care of the business. If he was running the business, he wasn't making any money. He was pretty much the only one that could really run it. One night I came home from the office and I got home around midnight.

Now, my dad is an early bird. He's usually up at 3:00 to 4:00 AM in the morning to start his route, for his vending machine business. But when I came home at midnight, I actually saw that my dad was already awake. He was still awake and was loading his truck with supplies. And this was very odd because my dad has to wake up so early that he's always in bed by, you know, nine o'clock, maybe 10 o'clock at the absolute latest. So, I approached him. I said, dad, like, why are you still up? Don't you have to get up early in the morning? And what he told me is that he was already awake, that he had started his day at midnight because he just had so much to do. And it was at that point that it really pulled at my heart. And I said, there's something that's not right with this picture.

I need to do something, because I want to be able to give back to my parents and to my dad and to help him retire. And so, that was when I truly understood the power of owning a business. It was one of the moments in my life, that really opened my eyes to the power of truly owning a business. But it ends.

But it really got me! It really shook me, because I said I need to do something. I need to be able to help my dad to retire so that he doesn't have to continue to do this. That's something that drives me and something that I want to do. Now that I've been a part of *World Financial Group*, my husband and I have been able to do amazing things. Things that we would've never been able to otherwise. But besides the money that we've made, besides the people that we've helped, besides the things that we've been able to do for our own family members, the thing that has definitely been the most rewarding part about this journey is the person that I've become through it.

It has helped me to become a better person in all areas of my life. It has helped me in setting goals, not just in my business world or the financial world, but also in my spiritual life. And that's something that I believe is just absolutely incredible. I'm so grateful that this company has provided for us.

One of the things that I learned while being in this business is that it's not easy, but it is simple. Part of the journey that I've discovered is that there's never really an end point in personal development. There's always a place to learn. There's always a place to grow. It's in those learning and growing moments and the journey itself where the true joy and appreciation lies.

Because of the way I hear success talked about, I've always

believed success equates to more money. But the meaning of success is so much more than that. It's about truly doing something where you're an inspiration to others and you're making a difference. Success means using your gifts to bring value to other people and to inspire other people to also utilize their gifts. Success means bringing value to the world while serving others. Fortunately, I found the best platform that allows me to do just that.

I am so grateful for the opportunity to be a part of this company and to continue to grow, to continue to help people with their financial education and to continue to transform people's lives into what is their "possible."

Kirsten Baron, (909) 908-4713,
Kbaron28@outlook.com

CARLOS ROJAS

My name is Carlos Rojas. I was born on August 21, 1984 and raised in Glendale, California. My parents migrated to the US from Mexico in the 80's. Both worked tremendously hard as factory workers earning $3 dollars/hour. We lived in a 1 bedroom, 500 square foot apartment that we shared with 3 aunts, four uncles, both my parents and 2 younger siblings. I remember me and my siblings sleeping on a bunk bed that was small enough to fit in a walk-in closet. I didn't know one could have their own bedroom, until I made friends and saw their homes. One of my childhood memories, was bundling up with my siblings and together praying while looking out through a small window in our closet.

I joined World Financial Group in October 2010. Although I worked at WFG, I still maintained a full-time job at a post-production company named Dyson Media. I was in charge of designing the layout for commercials at the company. I also did voiceover work that was included in the commercials. I was paid $640 net a week, $800 before taxes. I thought it was a great opportunity, especially after I had resigned from one of the Largest Land Planning and Development Consulting Firms in the Country, Hogle-Ireland. In 2007, I graduated from Cal Poly Pomona with a bachelor's degree in Urban and Regional Planning. I got hired to work for Hogle-Ireland in the summer of 2007, two weeks before my commencement ceremony. My parents couldn't be prouder. I couldn't be happier. I had spent thousands of dollars and countless hours earning my degree at Cal Poly. Three months after I began working for the firm, the market crashed. Development ceased. Developers and contractors stopped most of their projects. There was no work to be done in the planning sector. To make ends meet, I began working as a driver for an elderly day care center located in Sun Valley. I made $250 a week picking up seniors from their home and dropping them off at the center. I knew that I had hit rock bottom. Nothing at the time seemed to be going right. I was spending time with bad associations, drinking and partying 4 times a week in search of something that would fill a spiritual void. My parents and I were struggling financially. I was drastically in need of an opportunity. One of my neighbors told me about Dyson Media and that is where I met Ryan Ademy, who introduced me to World Financial Group.

My first year with WFG was very challenging. I was taking the bus from North Hollywood to Westlake Village. That was a two-hour commute. There were many times when I missed the second bus that I would catch in Woodland Hills. If I missed that bus, I would have to wait an entire hour for the next bus to come by. My two-hour commute would turn into a three-hour commute. It took me 7 months to get my license. Mainly because I struggled with the studying, and I took the license exam 7 times before I passed. It was difficult to express to my friends and family that this was an amazing opportunity. Most of the time, they saw me struggle. I knew somehow, in my spirit, that this opportunity would change my life. God had planted a seed of belief in my heart that he watered every-day with hope. I almost quit World Financial Group multiple times. I never understood why my family and friends were not as supportive as I imagined. They were the very reason why I was doing the business. I desired a better life for my parents and siblings, I wanted to set a great example. I wanted to grow and help everyone in my family grow. There were days when I would be on the bus an entire day going from appointment to appointment. Days when I would get up at 5am on a Saturday morning to get to office trainings at 9am. Days where I would walk to my appointments from the bus and be drenched from the rain. Days that I wished the wind would blow through my suit and offer a cool breeze on a hot summer day. Through the grace of God All Mighty and Knowing, I stayed with the business despite all of the adversity.

My vision of the future became brighter and clearer after I met the love of my life. I met Yvette Rojas in February of 2014. Soon came Emery Leah Rojas, our little princess, a gift from God. I knew immediately that my life was bigger than me. It was hard to miss Yvette, especially because her last name was also Rojas. She was so beautiful and just filled with dreams and tenacity. A new power couple was born. We began to get clear on everything we wanted for our lives and the people we wanted to become for our daughter, family and friends. Yvette and I hired two business coaches, read countless personal development, business and spiritual books, attended seminars and quickly aligned with who we wanted to become. The keys to personal success were no longer about what we had or how much money we made. It was more about who we were becoming.

The biggest lesson in life are: learning humility the hard way; knowing that at any moment anything can be taken from you; learning that knowing everything is knowing nothing at all; that an untried opportunity is more than a missed opportunity; that skepticism is not a bad thing; seek curiosity to learn the truth which can inspire one to try new things. I've learned that many want to change their lives, but few have the faith and courage to take the first step.

"Therefore I say to you, whatever things you ask when you pray, believe that you receive them, and you will have them."
Mark 11:24 NKJV

Carlos Rojas, (818) 674-9980,
carlosrojaswfg@gmail.com

YVETTE ROJAS

I clearly remember the night I sat in my 500-square-foot Hollywood studio, feeling defeated and dissatisfied with my life. I was begging the universe (or anyone up there that was listening) for an opportunity to take me out of my current situation. In my mind, I was a complete failure. Up until that point, I had graduated from Cal State University, Fullerton with a B.A in Communications and an emphasis in Entertainment Studies, believing that the movie industry is where I wanted to plant my career flag.

I moved to tinsel town a month after my college graduation, full of hope and excitement. I thought I was going to work backstage in films, help bring movies to life and rub shoulders with celebrities for a living. Almost 3 years had passed since that move, and so far I had nothing to show for it except for having assisted in the initiation of an acting school that failed, an "up and coming" TV show that went nowhere, and an extensive knowledge of deep tissue massage, since I'd resorted to getting a job as a receptionist in a spa because I needed the money.

My entire life, I was told to focus on school and get good grades so I could land a good-paying job. I always had an inkling towards entrepreneurship, but I knew nothing about running a business. And even if I *wanted* to start a business, "it takes money to make money," and from where exactly was I going to get all that money? What kind of business would I start? Who was going to help?

That painful night, I closed my eyes and prayed. I didn't know what to call my dream career, but I knew I wanted 3 things:

1. To be in control of my time and my life. I hated the idea of somebody telling me what to do, when to do it, and how much money my time is worth.

2. Make lots of money. I was sick and tired of struggling financially. My paychecks never made sense to me. How could I work long hours seemingly every day and still not earn enough to live decently?

3. Make a difference in other people's lives. Having worked in one of the most egocentric industries in the world, I realized very quickly that I would rather be a part of something that treats people with kindness. I

wanted to do something that would impact individuals in a positive way, perhaps even change their lives.

About a month after that night, I was invited by an ex-colleague and good friend of mine to a party at his house. That is where I met David and Hanna Horenstein, and my life would never be the same after that.

Through conversation, I learned that David was in search of an assistant to help him and Hanna manage their business. They worked in financial services, which I knew nothing about, and it had never occurred to me that this was an industry, let alone something I would ever want to be a part of. But at this point, I was open to almost any opportunity, and I jumped on it. I asked him to consider me and I told him I would drive anywhere necessary in order to land an interview.

The next day, he called and asked to meet for an initial interview. Of course I showed up. After that, the next step was to attend a meeting and get an overview of the company. On a cold Wednesday evening in February 2014, I showed up. As I checked into the meeting at the front desk, I was greeted by a gentleman with a big smile and a name badge that read "Carlos Rojas."

"I like your last name," I joked. As it turned out, my last name is Rojas, too.

I don't remember much about the presentation that evening, but I do remember leaving with a positive impression and feeling very excited. The next day, I was hired as a base shop coordinator (assistant) for the Horenstein base shop.

The first couple of months in my new position were rough. There were many growing pains. This was a foreign industry to me, and I had to figure out how to navigate a great deal of it on my own.

I am infinitely grateful to David and Hanna for having the confidence in me to push me the way they did. They trusted me with their business and although there were many times where I felt overwhelmed and uncertain, somehow I always managed to get it done. As a result, my confidence grew and I developed tremendous mental strength. I began to believe in myself once again, for the first time in a long time.

As the months passed, I learned more about WFG and the business opportunities that exist within the firm. Becoming an active agent that helps families become financially independent sounded intriguing. *Here it is!* I thought. *This is the opportunity I've been asking for!* WFG would allow me to have total control of my time, to work for myself, become financially independent, and to help a lot of other people achieve those same goals. I truly believe I was meant to join this company.

I had the advantage of learning the business from the inside out. The old me would have never given myself the opportunity to show myself what I could do, but the new me was up for the challenge.

I'm grateful we live by such strong principles in WFG because when I approached Hanna with my idea of getting licensed and becoming an agent, she enthusiastically encouraged it. I don't believe there are many companies where a boss would agree to train the assistant so that one day that assistant could reach their same level of success.

I continued to work full-time as an assistant in the office and began my training in WFG part-time. This required a lot of effort and many sacrifices. There were days where I would spend over twelve hours at the office, working my regular job from 9a.m. to 5 p.m. and then voluntarily staying for the training sessions from 6pm to 10pm. I set up my "field training" appointments during my off hours and weekends. As a result, I started ditching outings with my friends, and I constantly missed family events.

I understood that in order for my life to change, I needed to change. I continued showing up to every training session. I never missed a meeting. I immersed myself in personal development. I began working on shifting my mindset and stretching my vision of what (and who) I allowed myself to become. I developed a business plan, read books, listened to audiobooks, and attended countless training seminars, such as Tony Robbins' "Unleash the Power Within" and Steve Seibold's "Getting Rid of Approval Addiction."

My excitement caused my family to question me, and my friends started distancing themselves. They viewed my changes as negative because I was no longer available to them in the way they were used to. At first, this was very difficult for me, but the more I grew as a person, the more I realized the people I choose to surround myself with mattered. After all, you are the average of the five people you spend the most time with.

Funny enough, the person I enjoyed spending the most time with was my trainer, (now soon-to-be-husband) Carlos Rojas. I was immediately drawn to his excitement and positivity. We spent hours on the road traveling from appointment to appointment, and the time we spent together flew right by as we compared our dreams and goals and talked about what we needed to do to accomplish those dreams.

He taught me so much about this business and has always encouraged and praised me for my accomplishments. He believed in me like no one else. I grew smitten and our trainer/trainee relationship blossomed into love. It's been five years, and our partnership has never been stronger. In business, we joined forces as one power couple building a WFG army together. In life, we continue to grow as partners and parents to our beautiful three-year-old daughter, Emery Leah.

Carlos and I use the success principles we have learned over the years in every aspect of our lives. In faith, we strive to strengthen our personal relationship with our creator and foster gratitude for everything that we have. In family, we strengthen each other with encouragement, praise, and love.

In finances, we practice what we preach. Saving money on a monthly basis is non-negotiable, and our path to financial independence is clearly defined in our business plan. We work hard. It is our mission to add value to other people's lives in any way that we can. We are driven by our crusade to financially empower all families. "No family left behind" is our motto.

My biggest lesson throughout this journey has been that adversity is part of life, but "every adversity, every failure, every heartbreak, carries with it the seed of a greater or equal benefit." (Napoleon Hill, *"Think and Grow Rich"*) Adversity is simply an opportunity to learn and grow. It's important to remember that nothing happens *to* you, it happens *for* you.

It takes hard work and lots of failure to achieve greatness. When our daughter was born, we didn't know how the bills were going to get paid, but shortly after that, we earned $20,000 in one month. There have been lessons in every adversity and every blessing, and I'm grateful for all of them.

WFG has been a gift. I am not the same person I was six years ago when I first stepped into that presentation. I am still on the journey towards becoming the best possible version of myself, but as I look behind me, I am incredibly proud of how far I've traveled. I'm grateful for where I've been, and I'm excited to be on track to where I want to be. Your dreams are right around the corner if you have a plan, a system, and most importantly, God on your side. And "with God all things are possible."

Yvette Rojas, (619) 207-9861,
tenaciouswfg@gmail.com

Raul Julian Reyes, Jr.

Raul Julian Reyes, Jr. is the name that my father gave me. I am named after my father, and I received more than just his name. Before you can understand me, it is important to understand the people that created me as it has built the foundation for my character and who I am today.

Mr. Raul Reyes Sr. grew up in a small town in Mexico named Monte Escobedo, Zacatecas. The town had no running water and no electricity with very limited resources. The next town was about an hour away via car ride. To get to the next town, Huejucar, Jalisco, my grandparents had to take a horse or donkey through dangerous mountain ridges. Eventually, when cars were brought to the area, it made the adventure a little bit easier. To sum it up, my father came from the middle of nowhere, Mexico... Literally.

Despite the remoteness of his hometown and the limited access to resources, the Mexican culture was heavily ingrained in his DNA. My dad shared stories with me about his upbringing. Since as long as he can remember, people in his town knew how to do one thing, and one thing very well: party. Tequila, beer and good music were literally the only things that were necessary to start a party, and it could start anywhere, even in the middle of the street. My father learned how to be personable through his upbringing and have a good time, and to this day he approaches life with a very specific mindset. He brings witty jokes, loud laughs, and a big smile to even the dullest situation. To sum up my dad's outlook on life, it's a "life is short, so why not laugh" mentality. My dad came to the United States of America at age 16 and decided to bring an attitude of comedy, positivity, work ethic, and an overall attractive charisma with him to this country. He landed in Los Angeles, California, where he lived in a 1-bedroom apartment with 12 other family members. My uncle got him a gig at IHOP as a bus-boy, and he was ready to roll his sleeves up and get to work. His career at IHOP was short lived as his charisma attracted a very unique person to the restaurant: one of the directors of the Los Angeles Community College District. She liked my dad so much that she offered him a job with the City, and he proceeded to spend the next 40 years of his life working for the Los Angeles

Community College District.

While working at the college, my dad met a very special young lady named Susanna Paraja. This young lady was trying to study, but the man with the afro (my father) kept bugging her at the bus stop on her way home. And according to my mom, it was every single day. My dad apparently had a reputation of being a womanizer and had a very hard time persuading my mom to give him attention. But, one thing he was really good at was being witty and making her laugh. He wouldn't quit. Eventually, this young light skinned lady with big green eyes eventually let this funny Mexican with an enormous afro and thick chest hair take her out on a date. The date turned into a relationship, and the relationship led to a child; which according to my parents, ended up being the biggest blessing in their lives. But the relationship was built on rocky grounds, as my mother's upbringing was far different than that of my father's.

My mother is of Ecuadorian descent. My grandparents on my mother's side were both born and raised in Guayaquil, Ecuador. When my grandmother was pregnant with my mom, they decided to come to the United States. My mom was born in Chicago, Illinois. They then moved to Los Angeles where she ended up attending Middle School and eventually High School. My mother's household was volatile, as my grandfather was an army veteran with PTSD. He came back home with severe trauma and ended up bringing many of those traumas into the household. My mom grew up around a lot of anxiety and violence, and therefore it ended up severely affecting her mental health. My grandfather was always angry, and my grandmother worked 12 hours a day. My mother rarely saw her mom and was scared of her father. She wanted out of her house, and my dad was the key to a new life.

At the time, my father lived with my grandparents in a small apartment in a gang neighborhood in North Hollywood, California. My mom decided to move in, knowing it was a bad neighborhood, because all she wanted was to have a loving and caring family environment. My father, along with my grandparents, were able to provide that for her. Not far into living together, Baby Raul was born. Around the same time, my grandfather from my mother's side died. He was a heavy drinker, smoker, and loved to travel the world and eat good food. His tombstone reads, "Jose Paraja, loving father and husband, Army Veteran and epicurean." Epicurean means "pursuit of pleasure, especially in reference to food, comfort, and other luxuries. All concepts in Epicurean Lifestyle are based on the teachings of Ancient Greek philosopher Epicurus." He strongly believed that living a life full of simplicity was the way to achieve all the pleasure and comfort. My mom always said that aside from the smoking and drinking habits, and his horrible temper, that I remind her a lot of him. He was a strong militant man with huge green eyes and a bodybuilder physique who always made whatever came out of his mouth happen. He was a man of his word. His name was Jose, and his nickname was El Gato. I never got to meet him, but she said that all he wanted was to live a lifestyle full of travel, fun, good food, and good music. He loved Salsa Music and Motown, and apparently, I get my love of music from him. She still has his huge collection of records in storage. Unfortunately, his lifestyle affected his ability to live long enough to enjoy it for the long term.

The reason that this back story is so important is because

my personality and who I am at my core is a mix of my parents. My father is funny, witty, sharp, and a fast learner. His personality is amazing, and everyone likes him, but it comes at the expense of not taking life seriously. To this day, he has a f*** it attitude with almost everything. My mom, on the other hand, is conscious, competitive, well-spoken, extremely street smart, and fights for what she believes in. Her personality is that of a champion, but she has been debilitated her whole life by severe anxiety, a lot of which has to do with her upbringing. She is the type of person you either love or hate as she is extremely loving and empathetic, yet can get competitive and fierce in the blink of an eye. She has a hunger for travel, enjoys good food, and is constantly educating herself, a lot of what she picked up from my grandfather. I am fortunate to God that I picked up my father's ability to be sharp witted, quick with my tongue, quick with my learning, and likeable, in combination with my mom's competitive spirit, street smarts, and champion mentality. I am so fortunate that I did not pick up the severity of her anxiety, but I am also fortunate that I got to understand how crippling and serious it could be. Today, my mother is on disability from Los Angeles Unified School District, as her anxiety is so severe that it has crippled her to the point where she cannot work. I fight every day to make sure that I can be a positive impact on her and my father and provide to them what they have always wanted but never had the luxury of... a good quality of life. To give my mother the ability to see the world and leave her worries behind. To give my father the ability to know that he doesn't have to settle for a mediocre life and act like everything is perfect. To allow him the opportunity to do things he never had the money to do. That is part of the reason why I fight this fight in my life but not the entirety of it.

My earliest memories involve a loving family, in not so lovable conditions. The apartment was infested with rats and cockroaches. The gang members were friends with my father, again since he always made them laugh. My mom, on the other hand, was dealing with severe anxiety. Aside from losing her father, every night we would hear ambulances, gun shots, and all kinds of other craziness going on outside. The apartments were always covered with graffiti, and our neighbors' cars would constantly get broken into.

One night, our neighbor downstairs called the police on some of the gang members because they kept writing graffiti on his wall. The following night, he was shot and killed. At this point, my mom demanded my father move us out of that complex. My mother shared with me that as all the chaos was going on, she clearly remembers praying to God and making a wish. She asked, "God, my only wish to you is that you give my son the ability to be smart, make great decisions, and create a huge impact in this world."

My father worked a job that paid him very little income. My mother was a stay-at-home mom. How could they ever afford to move out of that apartment building and buy a house? Well, they put their thinking caps on and managed to borrow $10,000 in 1993 from my widowed grandmother. With this money, they managed to put a down payment on the cheapest house on the market, a few streets down from the apartment complex. In 1994, my Grandmother passed away during surgery, and my mother was left without her parents in her early 20's. We now had a house, which wasn't much better than the apartment building, and then the fighting ensued.

My father and mother would constantly get into arguments about money. My father couldn't afford anything outside of the mortgage, because he overcommitted financially to move us out of the apartments. My grandfather was the only other individual who brought in income. He provided a few hundred dollars a month from bussing tables at Bob's Big Boy. My father was what I later discovered to be "House Poor." He went through Chapter 7 Bankruptcy not once, but twice. We had a house, we had a place to lay our heads that wasn't as dangerous as our prior living conditions, but there was no longer a loving family. My grandmother and mother would clash. My father and mother would clash. It was a constant battle. Meanwhile, I minded my business playing Super Mario Bros., somewhat ignorant to what was happening. Every time I would see my mom crying, she would say, "I'm crying because I heard something funny that's all, I'm crying of laughter."

By the time I hit the 3rd grade, my mom and dad decided to break up. My mother had no stability and no family, so she went and tried to find another man to take care of her. My father had to take care of his parents since they had no money, so they moved back to an apartment building near the original complex, and this is where I was raised. My parents decided that staying with my father and mainly my grandparents, would be the best for me, as I would actually have a stable family to live with.

Growing up, I went to schools in low income neighborhoods. Money was always a problem. I had to do what I could to survive. I remember my friends and I from the apartment building would stand outside 7-11 and ask strangers for quarters. I also remember LAPD coming by during the holidays, popping their trunk and giving everyone in the neighborhood a toy. We shopped at a .98 store replicating the regular .99 store. I got so frustrated that I would buy chips and candies and sell them in the neighborhood for a profit. I was introduced to guns, drugs, and graffiti as the gang members went about their business. In my life, I have witnessed the deaths of three shooting victims, on different occasions, in the same neighborhood. I have witnessed people taking their last breath on the concrete floor.

My mother was not in a stable place in life, and I rarely saw her. My father was oblivious to the world and all the dangers around us. He worked most of the time and when he was home, he would relax and regenerate. Whenever I asked him why we didn't go anywhere or do anything, his answer was always, "no money". I grew up in the street with my friends, who were my role models. My centers of influence all came from broken homes. I didn't know any better.

My beliefs were that everything was normal. I thought shootings and stabbings happened everywhere. Gang members with nice cars and a lot of money were my success model. The graffiti artist who drew the coolest letters was the most talented. Deep down in my gut, I never felt right. I always walked home from school feeling anxious, like someone would come and get me, rob me, or pick a fight. Two kids recently had gotten shot and killed outside my high school, and I had that in the back of my head. I got into fights, and deep down inside, I didn't want to hurt anyone. I felt out of place with nowhere to run. I was the most conscious in the group, and when I would share deep thoughts and ideas, the others wouldn't follow the conversation. Everything around me was low level and I wondered why. I began to realize that I was different.

All odds were against me. I was meant to be unsuccessful. I was meant to get eaten up by the streets. I was meant to be average, or below average. But something deep down inside me, within the depth of my soul, screamed for more.

It's the same thing I carry with me today. This self-generated desire to break through and be big. This hunger to be successful. This engine that drove this machine. The machine didn't know where it was going, it just knew that it was going somewhere. It had no direction, no plan, no idea really. But it was ready to go and to go hard!

Something about my competitive nature automatically made me succeed in school. I saw tests and essays as a challenge. My mother put me in basketball teams growing up. I always wanted to be the best. I always wanted to score the most points. I always wanted to beat the other team. I realized that I wanted to be a winner. I never had a mentor to guide me, but anything life put in front of me, I wanted to win at it. Then... My life changed.

I finally found mentorship…and it was through music. I went from listening to friends and relatives to listening to Hip Hop. It spoke to me the most. It impacted my perspective and shifted my mindset. For the first time in my life, I had people that came from similar upbringings as I did sharing so much wisdom and knowledge through the form of music. I heard Jay-Z talk about business and his rise from poverty. I heard Notorious BIG talk about being the king and being #1 at his craft, exuding confidence. I heard 2pac poetically paint pictures of poverty. I became obsessed. I downloaded every single hip hop album that was relevant in the past 20 years. I became a student of the game.

Instead of going out in the street and being involved in gangs, I threw my headphones on, went to the gym, and played basketball. I had a rhyme book, where I started writing rhymes in the 9th grade. It was my sanctuary. I went from out of shape and flabby to strong and muscular. I went from average basketball player to the best scorer and defender on the team. I became well spoken. I went from being a spectator, to joining all the rap battles in the street and at school and being one of the best lyricists. I went from never having anything, to having an entire music studio in my room that I built from scratch.

Eventually, I went from gangs and poverty, guns and drama, to the University of California Santa Barbara. For the first time in my life, as silly as it sounds, I was around Caucasian people. I was in a safe place, where I could jog around the neighborhood and ride my bike at night. I interacted with people that were book smart, yet not very street smart.

It was awkward, different, but I loved it! It was something new! I could see the stars in the sky. The sky was no longer covered in smog... my vision became clear. I met an individual named Robert Claros during my first ever night out in Isla vista. We almost got into a fist fight. He didn't like me, and I definitely didn't like him. Ironically, we ended up becoming very close friends and fraternity brothers, and I realized that he was also from the "hood". He was from Pacoima. I was from North Hollywood. We started finding that we had more in common than we thought. He and I would play basketball almost every single day together and formed an awesome friendship. Upon graduating, I moved back home. The job market was tough for a 22-year-old kid out of college in 2011.

Robert and I reconnected through a basketball game. He said, "Hey, you're one of the smartest guys I know. I think you'd do good in financial services. I'm getting licensed to become a financial advisor right now, I actually work with two very successful financial advisors who manage a huge book of business."

What Robert didn't know was that for the previous 4 years, I had been obsessing about Finance and Economics. Aside from basketball and music, I craved to understand money and business. My parents had nothing, yet so many others seemed to have it all. My dad was always broke! My mom lost the house her parents left her because they had no estate plan. Because she lost that house, it would create an enormous ripple effect in her life and put us back an entire generation of wealth building.

To this day, my mother has nothing. I craved the answers. I wanted to learn about stocks, bonds, mutual funds, ETFs, insurance, and how to get ahead. I idolized businessmen like Jay-Z and wanted to be one myself; I just didn't know where to start.

During college, I had researched the top 10 careers in terms of pay, and Financial Advisor came up on the list. I also researched the top 10 careers in terms of happiness and Financial Advisor came up on the list. Robert had no idea that it was all destiny. He was one of the only guys in college that I truly got along with. He was also the only person that consistently played the sport I am so passionate about that also allowed us to reconnect. He also offered me an opportunity to work in a field that I had already been planning to enter.

A week before the basketball game where this discussion

took place, I had an interview with a major financial services company. I never went to the follow up interview. I would drive from North Hollywood to Alhambra for the next 6 months. I didn't get a job, I didn't get paid, but I was told that I could learn the business, and, if I got lucky, I could get sponsorship to get the coveted Series 7 License.

I shadowed the entire operation for months and would show up just to learn the business, hoping I would get an opportunity to take my test. Finally, the owner of the firm came to me and said "Raul, I see you're sharp, motivated, hungry, and passionate about this. I'm going to go ahead and open up your U4 window so you can go and take your test."

Six months after my first day in the office, I passed my exam on my first try. I was offered a full-time position with Padilla, Singh & Associates Wealth Management as a client services associate, aka Mr. Paper Pusher. I didn't mind it though because for the first time in my life, the machine finally had some direction. I was helping manage a business with $100,000,000 in assets under management. I started learning about money and business on a high level. My centers of influence started to change. My habits began to change. Within my first year, I went out and picked up my Series 66 License as well as my Life, Health & Accident insurance license. I was officially fully licensed. I was ready to conquer the world. But then reality hit me...

Big clients were not ready to trust a recently-licensed, 23-year-old Latino with their money. At least that is what I told myself. In reality, it wasn't that. I just didn't have the experience, knowledge, and abilities to connect and establish myself as a professional with this clientele. I also hadn't let go of the old me.

Shortly thereafter, I found my first real mentor: Shkira Singh. Shkira had 20+ years of experience in private wealth management and was a legend at a well-known US bank before going independent and starting her own business. She and her ex-husband ran a Million Dollar business; therefore, it was only right that I would follow her guidance. More importantly, she saw something in me that I am so grateful for. She saw the future me. The future me was vastly different than the Raul she met. She was up for a huge challenge in mentoring this young, stubborn bull into becoming a polished professional. Raul Julian Reyes Jr. Had all the intangibles. He was a quick learner, hungry, competitive, tenacious, and was ready to go to war, but Shkira made him see something that he was unable to see. He couldn't go to war with a slingshot.

I needed to grow and add weapons to my artillery. Then began the cleansing process, the personal growth process: The Landmark Forum; the Tony Robbins seminars; the retreats, the sound-baths, the sage, and the meditation. She helped me look in the mirror and realize that I had a victim mentality.

I thought I was perfect, and anytime anyone would tell me otherwise, I would battle them. I would point the finger and turn things around on people. I had an employee mindset. I felt that anytime things wouldn't go well, it was Padilla, Singh & Associates fault. Anytime I couldn't close a deal or find a new client to help, it was because PS&A didn't provide enough resources. When she or anyone else would criticize me, I would ask them to look in the mirror and criticize themselves. I was not coachable. I was a know-it-all. I felt that because of my life experiences and everything I went through, I deserved success and I deserved it fast.

I was mad... because I was working for advisors bringing in $1,000,000 a year. I was mad because all the staff was making more money than me. I was mad because I was out in the field all by myself trying to figure this thing out while making $1,000 a month. Shkira had a very hard time understanding me. We would constantly battle. Until I realized that the person I was really mad at was the person I was.

One day, Shkira asked me... "Raul, who do you idolize?" I said "Kobe Bryant". She then went and studied Kobe and went a step beyond and studied Phil Jackson. She started speaking my competitive language. She started opening my perspective to the reason why Kobe was successful. He wasn't successful because he was given anything, he was successful because he obsessed over his craft. He showed up early and left late. He became a master at what he does and made no excuses. A true competitor, who is widely respected for exactly those habits. I then realized that I needed to start performing more like Kobe Bryant and less like a fan.

Fast forward to January of 2018, I was let go from PS&A Wealth Management. The company was having internal struggles and ended up getting sold off. In my 6 years at the company, I never made more than $60,000 annually as an employee of the company. I was ready to go out and finally be on my own. I saw this as a huge blessing in disguise. There were certain toxic characteristics in the company that I didn't realize until far later that were limiting me from my true potential. Mainly, the comfort of a salary was my biggest enemy! Shkira guided me towards a lady by the name of Hanna Horenstein, who we met through the Tony Robbins seminar that I mentioned earlier.

I had offers from several major financial institutions, all of which you would have heard of. All offers provided a six-figure salary. I declined all and decided to partner up with Hanna Horenstein for one main reason: it was an opportunity to build a business for myself but not by myself. It was the key to financial freedom that I had been looking for. I could build a real business that would operate even when I am not around. I could leverage Hanna's expertise and the relationship she had established with Marshall Faulk and the NFL Alumni. I also had the opportunity to bring over some of my clients from the previous firm and build on those relationships.

In March 2018, I decided to make the move and get to work. It would become the best decision in my life up to this point. The Machine finally had real direction, and it was either sink or swim.

I was finally an entrepreneur. I had a business to build, and it was up to me and SOLELY me as to whether it succeeded or failed. Within my first year, I built my business to a high level and officially became a partner of Virtuity Financial Partners.

I finally have personal savings, I am a homeowner, and I have a thriving business with some of my closest friends. My personal and business relationships have transformed. I have more conviction about what I do now than ever before. With my previous firm, I could only help rich people get richer. I felt out of place as a young Latino with tattoos all over his body. I didn't have a platform to help every-day, average Joes. I remember trying to ask my previous boss to help my dad with retirement. He said, "I'll help him, but we will have to charge him $2000 for a financial plan." Today, we help all individuals from all walks of life get ahead financially without having to charge them for a financial plan. I work with doctors, lawyers, business owners, and engineers on a day-to-day basis on how to plan effectively, but I also have the ability to help the less-successful individuals get out of debt, create a plan for free, insure their family, and have a business opportunity that no one else will give them! I lead by example, walk the walk, and talk the talk. I have implemented the principles that I teach and feel qualified because 90% of the time, I have more money saved than they do when I learn about their finances, and I am only 30 years old! I am living proof that what we do works. I am not your average financial advisor. I am a product of the street. I am a product of immigrants and of a broken family. I am covered in tattoos. I am young and had rats and cockroaches in my household growing up. I wasn't supposed to advise people on their finances. Today, I am a major asset to my clients, a difference maker in my team's life. I am building a well-rounded practice where my clients have confidence that their advisor is completely unbiased and can help them with strategies to improve their financial life, all the while building a team of fully licensed individuals who can do the same for their clients. I am able to speak with street smarts and intuition just as much as I am able to speak with book smarts. With almost a decade of experience in financial services, and 30 years of experience in the school of hard knocks, you won't find another Raul Reyes like this one. I doubt there is another financial advisor out their like me.

I can converse with the youth in the streets and can acquire a multimillion-dollar 401(k) plan in the same day. I can create beautiful music and establish a tax-free retirement plan for a client. I can score 30 points in a basketball game and help an individual create a new stream of income at the same time. I have a deeper level of consciousness than most people and will recreate myself in each and every single one of my teammates. My family loves me and is proud of me. My clients value me and trust me. My prospective clients that I haven't met yet are in for a treat. The team that I mentor is in for a life changing experience. "We are just getting started."

I came from a broken family; it was supposed to provoke insanity.

But God had something planned for me. First, I had to stare into the broken vanity.

Never was I taught money management or business and most of my family is in money prison.

Using the credit, they love to give us, buying the Gucci and Louie that doesn't fit us.

All to impress these people that don't serve us,

Habits will keep you poor and serving burgers,

Inside they rotten outside a superb surface,

Can't understand it, we live in the worst circus.

Digging ourselves into bigger holes, putting your figures in figure fours.

You gotta step into these bigger roles, to have the Rolls Royce outside of the bigger homes.

My mother was getting desperate, told my father you gotta make an investment,

We leaving these buildings making exit,

Our neighbors are bleeding every evening getting they head split.

New home not much has grown since, we still living among the homeless.

We Ain't living among the Jones's, too much killings we living among the hopeless.

I gotta step up and make a change, shift the mindset where you grind just to pay for chains.

Modern day slaves in cages it stays the same, from all the toxins around you that fill your brain.

From all the bad habits and debt that fills the banks, do the opposite watch your wallet get filled with franks.

Be the best at it every time they reveal the ranks, set my family free so they really can feel the thanks.

Raul Julian Reyes, Jr., (818) 588-9323,
rjulianreyes@yahoo.com

www.ingramcontent.com/pod-product-compliance
Lightning Source LLC
Chambersburg PA
CBHW071646210326
41597CB00017B/2135